The Balanced Child

Teaching Children and Students the Gifts of Social Skills

Brett Novick

ROWMAN & LITTLEFIELD
Lanham • Boulder • New York • London

Published by Rowman & Littlefield
An imprint of The Rowman & Littlefield Publishing Group, Inc.
4501 Forbes Boulevard, Suite 200, Lanham, Maryland 20706
https://rowman.com

Unit A, Whitacre Mews, 26-34 Stannary Street, London SE11 4AB,
United Kingdom

Copyright © 2018 by Brett Novick

All rights reserved. No part of this book may be reproduced in any form or by any electronic or mechanical means, including information storage and retrieval systems, without written permission from the publisher, except by a reviewer who may quote passages in a review.

British Library Cataloguing in Publication Information Available

Library of Congress Cataloging-in-Publication Data Available

ISBN 978-1-4758-3986-9 (cloth: alk. paper)
ISBN 978-1-4758-3987-6 (pbk.: alk. paper)
ISBN 978-1-4758-3988-3 (ebook)

∞ ™ The paper used in this publication meets the minimum requirements of American National Standard for Information Sciences Permanence of Paper for Printed Library Materials, ANSI/NISO Z39.48-1992.

Printed in the United States of America

I would like to dedicate this book to my late father, Dr. William Novick, who taught me how to be a father. To my parents who taught me the importance of hard work and values. My wife, Darla, who teaches me each and every day how to be a better person, parent, and spouse. My children, Billy and Samantha, who give me hope for a future generation with pride. Also, to the many students, parents, and educators that I have had the honor of working with over the years who have taught me so very much. Please know I am honored to be allowed to play a small part in their lives. The many mentors who in both education and life inspired me in every aspect of my life. Finally, a heartfelt thank-you to the publishers and staff at Rowman & Littlefield for your confidence in publishing this book and you, the reader, for taking precious time out of your schedule to read my book. Thank you.

Contents

Introduction: The Trouble with Social Skills — vii

1. Anger, the Emotion with Strong Roots — 1
2. It's Not My Fault!: Encouraging Responsibility in Our Children — 13
3. There Is a Big World Out There: Practical Social Skills — 31
4. A Walk in Someone Else's Shoes: Helping to Develop Compassion and Empathy — 47
5. We're All the Same: Teaching Our Children to Dive into the Melting Pot of Tolerance — 57
6. Making a Good First, Second, and Third Impression: The Importance of Hygiene — 65
7. Fishing for Friends: A Hard Catch — 71
8. Agreeing to Disagree: Conflict Resolution Skills — 83
9. Entering the Workforce and Beyond: Growing to Adulthood — 91

Conclusion — 97
Appendix — 99
Index — 103
About the Author — 107

Introduction

The Trouble with Social Skills

We're losing social skills, the human interaction skills, how to read a person's mood, to read their body language, how to be patient until the moment is right to make or press a point. Too much exclusive use of electronic information dehumanizes what is a very, very important part of community life and living together. —Vincent Nichols

CHILD PROFILE

On a beautiful fall day, Johnny[1] runs out to recess with the leaves crunching under his feet. The crisp autumn air is whistling in his ears. He is happy as the cold October rains pouring for the past several days have caused everyone to be indoors for recess.

The playground is full of potential playmates. They are all scurrying about to begin games of football or tag and climbing on the playground equipment. He scans the large field and finds several students beginning a football game. He runs over, almost knocking the other children over in his excitement. Johnny blurts out, "Can I play?" The children gathered together in a huddle ignore his first request. He asks again, this time louder, "Hey, can I play?" Again, the children provide no response as they are reviewing who is going to be on what team.

Johnny's face becomes reddened with the anger of having been ignored. He thinks, "These kids hate me. . . . They are not wanting to play with me! I am going to show them!" As the football game begins and all the children line up clumsily, Johnny jumps in front of the ball. "I am playing! You are going to let me play!" In doing so, he accidentally knocks over some of those very kids with whom he wants to play and they are quick to tell the teacher.

The teacher runs over to the area where the commotion continues to brew under the rustling of the leaves and the fumbling for the football. "What is going on here?" the teacher asks in a huff. All the children turn toward Johnny, who is now crying and embarrassed to have been pointed out by the group of which he so badly wanted to be a part.

Johnny is well known to the teacher. He is the kid that always gets in trouble, the one who never seems to fit, the perpetual square peg in a round hole. "Why did you push and hit them?" Johnny thinks about it and gives a perhaps all-too-honest answer: "Because they did not want to play with me!"

As the teacher stares suspiciously at Johnny and his direct and honest pronouncement, he impatiently tells Johnny, "Come with me!" Johnny now finds himself in the office of the assistant principal. In this place, he has memorized every picture, every degree on the wall, and every grain of wood on the aging desk. "You again?" the administrator asks, half as a question but more as a statement. "You obviously need to learn how to get along with others. You need to see Mrs. Clark."

Mrs. Clark is the school counselor; Johnny also has her room memorized. Children's bright drawings adorn the walls, along with games that have faces of children that are happy, sad, mad, and glad. There is a long table, with clay, paints, and paper scattered along it, where Johnny sits. Mrs. Clark sits with a soft, almost inaudible voice and whispers, "We are going to learn social skills: how to make friends."

They sit, they play games, they talk about what are friends, they rehearse, and then Johnny leaves the room. He feels good, now equipped to make new friends and to become popular, and dreams of having someone come over to his house. After all, he does not have to continue to play that one-player version of the newest video game that he got last Christmas. He wants to have a sleepover, to do the everyday things that mark the passages of childhood and make for wonderful dreams to look back on and treasure.

Except when he goes back and tries what he has learned at the playground, he runs into that same wall of rejection. Each day, it is like "Groundhog's Day" for him: rejection . . . try . . . rejection . . . try . . . rejection . . . try . . . give up trying to make friendships and socializing with others.

WHY THIS BOOK?

The world is a very lonely place for children who have challenges socializing. They go to schools with hundreds, or even thousands, of peers and yet they are most alone in those environments. These are the members of the next generation who, by their nature, are either on the periphery of their peer groups or become known for their awkward manner of attempting to get others to interact with them.

They have a limited scope of social skills tools in their proverbial tool belt. So, when a new or novel social opportunity comes up and they reach deep into the pockets of that tool belt, they come up short. They take whatever ill-fitting tool they find and try to use it in hopes it will work.

The problem is, if you have only a limited amount of tools, as the saying goes, "everything begins to look like a nail." So you try to smash that nail into the wall even if the only tool you may have is a screwdriver. When it does not work you think, try harder, louder, harder. In turn, you bend the screw or break the drywall altogether. Some of our children just need more tools to master.

As Benjamin Franklin once said, "Tell me and I forget, teach me and I may remember, involve me and I learn." It is involvement in actual social experiences that teaches children and that gets them to learn. Unfortunately, children with challenges in social skills seem to have an uncanny ability to "compartmentalize" skills. That is, they can use a skill in one area and then either overuse it in another scenario or not utilize it at all when it is warranted.

This book is short on theory and long on practicality as a consequence. It is, after all, a practical attempt at application of interactional skills in society, skills that are ever changing like the winds in these frenetic times that our next generation is living in and that will continue to shift ever more as we look toward the future.

Is this book for educators, counselors, or parents? The answer, quite simply, is yes. It takes the whole village of persons in the life of a child struggling with social skills for maximum synergistic effect. For each party that is not a part of it, the effectiveness is proportionally diminished accordingly. What we discuss here is for the parent who is their child's primary teacher, the educator who is the teacher, and the school counselor who is defined as a teacher of life skills. It takes one and all.

THE DESTRUCTION OF SOCIAL SKILLS

Only a decade or two ago, children could be found crowding the streets of suburban neighborhoods. They would be scurrying around hurriedly on bicycles, the sounds of a game of pickup football echoed between homes, and games of every conceivable type of "tag" were made up.

On the rainy days, kids could be found building things, talking to their friends on the phone, going to the mall to "hang out," or simply watching the rain trickle down in little trails on the window until the first peaks of sunlight allowed them to go outside.

Those days are gone somewhat. The streets are eerily quiet, deserted without the sounds of children laughing, the pattering of feet on the grass, and the clanking of bicycle pedals. They are now replaced by the simulated sounds of video racing cars, shooting of assault rifles, and the click clack of texts upon the small glass surfaces of smartphones.

Even when children are outside or go to the mall, they are transfixed by the soft white glow of smartphones. Children who are only a few inches apart are busily texting each other, when simply lifting their heads and speaking would be more effective and easier. Children now measure friendships not by who can sleep over at their house but by who is a friend on social media or willing to play interactive games via the Internet.

SO, WHAT IS THE BIG DEAL?

Socialization is a fundamental foundation for success. Each and every day, whether we like it or not, we are forced to socialize with others, from getting a pack of gum to working on large-scale projects at work. Socialization as an adult is a job duty that is subtlety embedded in each and every one of our lives and lifestyles.

True, some of us may be more introverted than others, and that is fine as well as vital. However, we must all have the ability to socialize when needed to get our needs (and the needs of those who depend on us) fulfilled. According to research at Concordia University in Irvine, California, children born since 1990 have "almost 80 percent fewer instances of social interaction in elementary school than previous generations."[2]

From the outset of our lives, we learn via socialization practice. We try what works; if it fails, we try a differing strategy. If we do not have opportunities to "flex our social muscle," we do not build that interactional part of us that is what makes us most fulfilled. Social skills don't come naturally; they are fortified on a foundation of trial and error. So what happens when social skills are not tested and learned?

THE DANGER OF POOR SOCIAL SKILLS

Children who do not have developed social skills find themselves in a world that is very difficult to navigate. If you do not have socialization abilities, how do you make friendships? If you cannot talk to people, how do you eventually go on a job interview? If you cannot advocate for yourself, how do you stand up to the playground bully? The questions go on and on, and each leads back to the trail of social skills.

The inevitable conflict that arises as children (and adults) disagree with each other becomes a challenge. According to an article in the *Huffington Post*, "Children become unable to handle conflict face to face because so much of their interactions occur through some sort of technology."[3]

RESEARCH ON SOCIAL SKILLS

Dr. Albert Mehrabian, author of *Silent Messages*, found that "7 percent of any interaction is conveyed through words."[4] That leaves a full 93 percent of communication that is relayed through tone and nonverbal body language and cues. Why is this important? Because if your child is not learning these other skills in communication (which is difficult with solely technological dialogue), it becomes virtually impossible to discern a whole message.

A collaborative study by Penn State and Duke Universities followed children from kindergarten to adulthood and scaled them throughout this time for their aptitude for socialization and social skills. "Those that had the stronger social skills scores were found to be 54% more likely to earn a high school diploma, and twice as likely to attain a college degree as well as 46% more likely to have a full-time job at age 25."[5]

Bolstering social skills also enriches a student's abilities academically. For instance, in the journal *Child Development*, researchers led by Joseph A. Durlak, at the University of Chicago, determined that "pupils who took part in social skills curriculum, improved on standardized-test scores by 11 percentile points versus other students."[6]

In a study by Don W. Jordan and Joanna Le Metais, they found that even ten weeks of social skill instruction showed evidence of socialization improvement.[7] Students were able to get along with others and even work in groups with those with whom they had initially had conflict. In short, they learned the ability to cooperate with those with divergent opinions and viewpoints. How often do we have to work with others that have views that we do not necessarily agree with or outright find objectionable? The answer to how you handle that scenario largely determines your vocational success.

THE FOUNDATIONS OF SOCIAL SKILLS

Social skills are a complex series of traits to learn and assimilate. After all, each and every one of us develops these skills through our lifetime. Social abilities are navigated and slightly changed each and every day of our lives (though we have a large basic foundation of what we utilize). Even those who are relatively adept at social interactions can pick up a host of self-help books and software applications that give means of sharpening already adequate social skills.

Let's talk for a moment, however, about what are the foundational social skills. Out of these traits, a child will build the scaffold framework from which to develop a longer-range set of social abilities as they develop into adulthood and beyond.

Here are the important social skills foundational traits that we will look at in this writing:

- Anger Management: Children must learn to look at, handle, and address anger in an assertive and productive manner.
- Practical Social Skills: Demonstrating that social skills are practical and applicable to the student/child so that they make sense in the world in which they reside.
- Empathy/Looking at the Other Point of View: This is, quite simply, the ability to put your feet in someone else's shoes, to look at another's perspective and look at a situation through their eyes and viewpoint.
- Developing Friendships: Children have many acquaintances that they encounter throughout their days and lives. How and where do they find and foster these connections into meaningful friendships?
- Conflict Resolution: Some children fall along a spectrum of aggression or passivity when discord arises. The passive child harbors anger at themselves because they did not advocate for themselves, but the flames of rage that a child uses to beat down disagreement are not useful. Assertive

abilities to stand up for yourself and what you believe in are far more effective and efficient tools.
- Ability to Listen/Communicating Effectively: The ability to listen, comprehend, and understand is a skill in this subset. Many children "hear" but do not "listen" to what the words truly say. The belief of using both ears instead of their one mouth falls neatly into this domain.

  As children grow and increase their verbal prowess so should their abilities to tactfully speak their mind and interact with others. Without the ability to get their point across in some efficient and effective manner, children often find that in school, in relationships, and vocationally they flounder in trying to get their message out to the world.
- Tolerance: In the Internet atmosphere of today, the globe is ever flattening. More and more children are going to have to work shoulder to shoulder with persons of varying cultures, languages, and viewpoints. An inability to understand and cooperate with those that differ from yourself places you in a precarious position.
- Ability to Assume Responsibility: Children readily assume responsibility for their positive actions. Yet, some of those same youth will point their mistakes at the feet of their parents, peers, educators, or supervisors.
- Hygiene Awareness: While perhaps not always a specified social skill, the ability to be presentable and care for oneself is a necessary part of being able to reach toward the best socialization potential.
- Vocational Skills: The workplace is an idiosyncratic microcosm that balances work with elements of socialization. It takes a careful mix to assure success in the job role.
- Dating Skills: The subject of dating is a most delicate homeostasis. It requires communication of affection without stepping over the invisible line of discomfort or inappropriateness.

NOTES

1. All children's profiles and situations contained within this book are purely fictitious.
2. Matthew Jones, "Smartphones Bad for Children's Social Skills?" *Razorback Reporter*, September 28, 2015, http://razorbackreporter.uark.edu/2013/12/smartphones-bad-for-childrens-social-skills.
3. Rachel Moss, "How Technology Is Having a Serious Impact on Your Child's Development," *HuffPost UK*, September 15, 2014, http://www.huffingtonpost.co.uk/2014/09/15/children-technology-impact-addiction_n_5821492.html.
4. Albert Mehrabian, *Silent Messages: Implicit Communication of Emotions and Attitudes*, 2nd ed. (Belmont, CA: Wadsworth, 1980).

5. Victoria M. Indivero, "Early Prosocial Behavior Good Predictor of Kids' Future," *Penn State News*, July 28, 2015, http://news.psu.edu/story/364050/2015/07/28/research/early-prosocial-behavior-good-predictor-kids-future.

6. Betty Ray, "Study: Promoting Students' Personal and Social Development Boosts Academic Outcomes, a Guest Blog by Joseph Durlak," *Edutopia*, March 23, 2011, https://www.edutopia.org/blog/social-emotional-learning-learning-boosts-academic-outcomes-joseph-durlak.

7. Don W. Jordan and Joanna Le Métais, "Social Skilling through Cooperative Learning," *Educational Research* 39, no. 1 (1997): 3–21, doi:10.1080/0013188970390101.

Chapter One

Anger, the Emotion with Strong Roots

> Education is the ability to listen to almost anything without losing your temper or your self-confidence. —Robert Frost

CHILD PROFILE

Rick is a fifteen-year-old teen who just got a job working as a dishwasher in the kitchen of a local nursing home. His boss, Mary, is a hard-nosed lady who often screams and yells in harsh tones at no one in particular. The work is dirty; hot water clouded with mashed potatoes and corn splashes on his apron, which is stained with the soup du jour and other foods that are splattered like paints on his white uniform.

Rick likes his coworkers; they tend to joke around and spray each other with the faucets and slide along the wet tile floors into each other. Rick laughs a too-loud belly laugh that gains the attention of his colleagues. He takes the spray hose that he has grasped in his hand and aims it at the others and gleefully pulls the trigger.

At first his coworkers chuckle in amusement. After a minute or so of getting soaked, they turn toward Rick and laughing turns to pleading that he stop so that they can get back to work ahead of the busy lunch rush. Rick is having fun; he feels he is finally being accepted by and amusing those he desperately wants to befriend so he continues to grip the sprayer and laugh with tears in his eyes.

The commotion attracts the ire of Mary who is no-nonsense and efficient. "Rick, stop playing around; get to work now!" He is now so thoroughly enjoying his time that he does not hear her loud utterances. She walks over to him; they are now nose to nose. She raises her voice even higher: "Get to work now!"

Her snarling voice snaps Rick back to attention. As he turns to her, she continues to yell and berate him about his lack of work ethic and how he "always has to carry things too far." As he watches her yell and drops of spit fly from her mouth, he feels the heat of rage begin to climb up his neck and into his clenched jaws.

"Screw you!" he yells. "You are a fat pig and I hate you! You're a jerk!" His colleagues try to settle him down, recognizing his job is now in peril. Yet, he continues, "No! I am not going to calm down! You are a horrible boss! You are never any fun . . . and you are always yelling and telling us what to do!" Rick feels the words spilling out of his mouth in rage. They are no longer within his control as they pour out in a stream of frustration.

Mary backs away, stunned by his insubordinate nature. "You, my friend, are fired!"

Rick now backs up, as if punched in the gut. "What?" he asks in stunned confusion.

"You are fired; grab your things and get out of here!"

Rick walks out without getting any of his personal materials and cries as he now has to go home to explain to his parents how he lost his third job.

TRIGGERS OF ANGER

It is important first to know and educate children on what are their triggers for potential anger. Knowing these prompts helps to recognize and somewhat inoculate the youth when these issues arise.

Situations, personal interactions, or even environments can spark the fire of rage to burn in a child/adolescent.

Common Interactional Triggers

1. Perspective of someone being rude to the child: If a child believes that someone is not respecting their rights as a person, they may lash out.
2. Joking/sarcasm: Those that have social deficits don't get the subtle vocabulary of "joking/sarcasm." As a result, they take everything at "face value" and not in the intent that the peer (or adult) intended.

3. People who are too loud or don't respect personal space: This is one that may seem counterintuitive. Many of those who are having trouble with socialization aspects often have challenges with being too loud and/or invading others' personal space. Yet, they also are aware and aggravated by peers who demonstrate similar behaviors to them.

Common Environmental Triggers

1. Having to wait: Many times these children have less of an attention span and ability to be patient compared to others. Being aware that they may have to wait, and knowing the approximate time for having to do so, provide a youth some control in this area.
2. Not being invited: In the world of youth, not being invited to a party or event is a huge rejection that is amplified via discussion of the occurrence via social media.
3. Perceiving academic failure in the school setting: If a child is failing at school, it is the equivalent of failing at their job and results in frustration or apathy.
4. Being overwhelmed by an environment: Look at your average large box store. Notice that the candy bars are located precariously at the eye level of most children and at the front of the store. The hope is that a child will be overwhelmed and snared by the candy. In turn, the parent will purchase the sweets versus risk the public shame of a tantrum.

Common Situational Triggers

1. New places that are not structured: The most difficult times for children are in places that are not structured and require them to test their limited social skills. These are times such as lunch, leisure time, parties/events, or any period where adults are not as available to provide boundaries and direction(s).
2. The subject of peers talking about you (or perceiving this): Youth can be mean to each other. The world of school can be one of gossip, rumors, and innuendo. If a child believes that they are being talked about or judged, this leads to anger. Keep in mind, however, that their perception may be inaccurate or have no merit (if they are simply assuming that this may be the case).

3. Unrecognized physical issues: Like an adult, if a child is hungry, tired, or ill, these lead to a youth having a reciprocally shorter temper. For those with good social and verbal skills, they can indicate that this is the case. Those who have challenges socially or with emotional regulation can be impaired from the ability to recognize this and subsequently tell others around them what they need.

ANGER HAS DEEPER ROOTS

Often children, and adults for that matter, experience anger as a singular emotion. However, anger is not that simplistic a concept. It is a blend of additional emotions such as fear, sadness, frustration, or even physical pain.

This is not always obvious to youth. They see anger as a singular emotion. It is the role of adults to act as the conduit to help them recognize that the "white-hot light" of anger has a spectrum of potential emotions that can be identified.

For instance:

- Rob is rejected by a peer group. He begins to yell and scream at those around him. He believes the issue is anger. In reality, the emotional contexts are also those of frustration (that he cannot get them to befriend him) and sadness (that they do not want to be his friend).
- Joe has been removed from his classroom due to his disruptive behavior. He is returned back to class and his teacher snarls, "Are you going to behave now?" He looks at all of his peers glaring at him and screams back to her, "Screw you!" (He is embarrassed and anxious.)
- Maria comes home furious. Her parents ask her what the matter is. She screams at them for no apparent reason. (Parents come to find out that she was rejected by a group of girls she wanted to befriend.)

Anxiety Can Be the Wolf in Sheep's Clothing

If a youth has social issues, when they enter the potentially anxiety-ridden environment of interaction with peers, this creates an ever-rising level of worry and fear. This discomfort is misread as that of anger solely.

Anxiety has a dual relationship. We must remember that anxious behavior has two parts that function in tandem. First is what they are saying in their brain (e.g., "I hate those kids"). Second, there is the reaction of the body or the so-called fight or flight reaction.

Extreme Anger Leads to Extreme Tunnel Vision

Remember a time when you were enraged. I mean a time when you felt your heart beating through your ears and your veins throbbed with the fuel of anger. Let's take the example of road rage, when someone cuts you off on the highway. Your sole focus is now on the "jerk" that has almost ended your life in an instant. You scream and use profanity that would make a trucker blush at the hapless car that speeds ahead (unaware that they have wronged you). At this time, it is a challenge for anyone to settle you down and you are incapable of listening to any strategies to do so because of your tunnel vision.

So it is with youngsters with poor social skills. When they have reached the point of rage, all the ideas and strategies that they have been building are thrown out the proverbial window. They are now myopically focused on the issue/person/situation at hand. You might say then, "Well, how do we work with children who will not remember anything we told them?"

The trick is to help the youth to notice when they are going from mild irritability, to frustration, to anger, then rage. We can reach them up to the point between anger and rage; however, once the point of rage is reached, it is like trying to put lava back into a volcano. So we must help them look for the sign and symptoms of anger that they may notice such as

- feeling "hot" on your face and hands
- clenching your jaw or biting your lip or tongue
- headache
- stomachache
- shaking
- feeling dizzy
- rapid heartbeat
- crying
- heavy breathing
- pacing around room

If a child is feeling these traits frequently, it is also an excellent idea to take them to the pediatrician to rule out the possibility that these are symptoms of an underlying medical issue.

THE BLACK AND WHITE OF FAIRNESS

Children tend to be very rigid in their understanding of fairness. They believe that "fair means equal." As we all well know, the concept of equality in the adult world is simply not possible. People working the same job have different salaries; some of us have advantages that others do not. Or, as Rod Stewart put in his classic 1970s ballad, "Some Guys Have All the Luck."

If we are going to teach youth a more accurate life lesson for fairness, it must be that "everyone gets what they need . . . not necessarily what they want." If this is not instilled, youth tend to make endless comparisons between what they have and what they assume their peers have. This sets the sights for frustration and anger that can never be quenched because they always see someone who has more than them, and jealousy will constantly rear its ugly head in their lives as a result.

ANGER EXISTS ALONG A CONTINUUM

The goal for anger is that of assertiveness, meaning that children have the ability to stand up for themselves when necessary and needed. This means that they are not overly passive and do not let everyone walk all over them. On the flip side, it does not mean that they are going to use aggression and be assaultive toward those around them (figure 1.1).

Either extreme has consequences. Those that are passive become down on themselves or may even "explode" with eventual pent-up anger. Those that are aggressive become known as "bullies or behavioral problems" and develop a reputation that is often a tailspin that is difficult to pull out of.

DEALING WITH ANGER

Fire . . . Ready . . . Aim

Children with social skills deficits often speak, or act, before they think. This leads to impulsive behaviors and gets them into difficulties before they even recognize they are in hot water.

Having them count to ten before they say something is simplistic; however, it can help keep them from experiencing verbal "diarrhea" of sorts, in which the words that come out of their mouth are not fully formed and are tinged with emotion versus tactfulness.

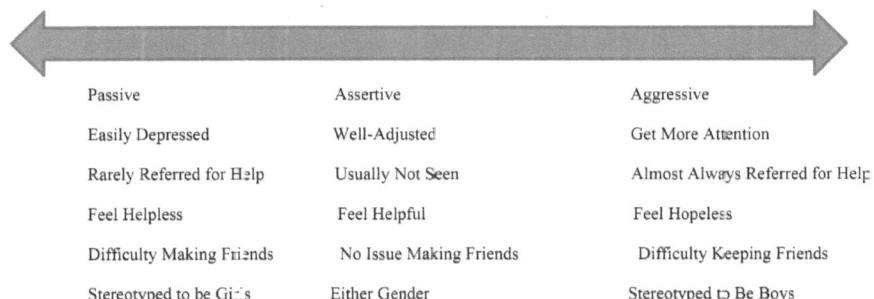

Figure 1.1. Anger Continuum

Lowering the Anger Threshold

While debate exists among professionals, it seems that prolonged exposure to violent video games, television shows, or movies may lead to a lower threshold for anger or frustration. Simultaneously, the repetitive watching/playing of this media may increase the likelihood of violent reaction to conflict in real life.

Walk Away

When a child is angry, as mentioned earlier, they have significantly lowered abilities to verbalize and to access the interventional tools at their disposal. Therefore, simply walking away and not addressing the issue are, perhaps, the easiest and most effective means of doing so.

The question then becomes, how long should they stay away from the source of their irritation? According to Dr. Daniel Goleman, author of *Emotional Intelligence*, it can take twenty minutes for one to fully recover physiologically from anger after the individual is no longer neurologically impacted.[1] In other words, once you see that the child is no longer mentally irritated, it takes another twenty minutes for their bodily thermostat to go back to its normal "temperature" (so to speak).

Teach Them the Importance of Being Funny

Sometimes the easiest way to diffuse the anger of a youth that is building toward the geyser of rage is humor. Doing something funny or teaching them to "laugh at themselves" avoids a harsh conflict in which they burn a potential bridge of social connection.

Change the Environment

If a youth is upset in a particular setting (e.g., the classroom, basketball game, home environment), sometimes just changing the environment to get fresh air can be all that is needed.

Check for Hungry, Tired, Ill

A child that has challenges socially also may have a comparable lack of bodily awareness. Look to see if the above issues are of concern; fulfilling those may be the missing piece to improving the child's mood.

Music

Music can tame the savage beast of anger. Giving a child a pair of headphones with relaxing music can help "tune out" the notes of anger that irritate them. Additionally, just using sound-canceling headphones, in conjunction with deep breathing or guided imagery, can help cease the drone of annoyance that is interfering with their ability to think in a clear fashion.

Scaling Anger

All of us have various levels of anger. They go from mildly irritated to furious. It is important to note and "scale" anger as a means of letting those around you know just how much of an issue the anger is and how to address it based on intensity (such as 1 calm to 10 furious).

If You Are Angry, There Are Rules

Youth often think that anger is not an appropriate emotion. They associate anger with rage or destructive behaviors. In reality, anger is a useful emotion that (in the correct context) can allow a child to solve problems and find their voice in the world.

That being said, it is important to point out some simple rules of anger:

1. You are not permitted to be destructive to other people's things.
2. You are not permitted to be mean to another in expressing your viewpoint.

3. You are not permitted to be mean to yourself. (This is perhaps the most vital because a child will often attack themselves verbally and incredibly harshly. In doing so, they attack an already fragile self-esteem via "beating themselves up." This anger turned inside out can lead to their feeling depressed about their own outlook on life.)

SEARCHING FOR POTENTIAL SOLUTIONS

As parents and educators, it is vital that we coach children along to potential solutions as well as the cause and effect relationship that each may have accordingly. In an article entitled, "The Teen Brain: It's Just Not Grown Up Yet," by Richard Knox, "Recent studies show that neural insulation isn't complete until the mid-20s."[2] The part that is not fully complete is the frontal lobe.

According to the website *Healthline*, "The frontal lobe is the part of the brain that controls important cognitive skills in humans, such as emotional expression, problem solving, memory, language, judgment."[3] This means when we ask a child, "What were you thinking?" they really may have had an inability to think and ponder fully the potential consequences of an action.

It may then be absolutely necessary for an adult to provide the information necessary for youth to make a "whole brain" and informed decision that they may not be fully capable of on their own.

Applications in Schools

Unfortunately, sometimes when media report on the issue of anger in schools, it is portrayed with issues of violence: a student (or group of students) who have been bullied or labeled as outcasts attempts to exact revenge on their educational community.

These students are often the ones who "fly under the radar." They may exist outside the fringe of the school community. They are often, real or imagined, the victims of bullying or harassment via the other students of the school body. Yet the services of school counseling or educational support are often not yielded to the fullest extent to them.

These students turn their anger and resentment inward. They do not develop the social skills necessary to become a part of some positive part of the school climate and continue to stew as a result. Hence, it is the students who are passive and suffering quietly from the turmoil of not feeling they have the school community to fall back on that should be sought. Looking for those who retreat into themselves and have few support outlets, as much as those who outright exhibit anger, is critical to help all in need of assistance with anger management.

Additionally, teaching assertiveness skills when they are most needed is of use for all students. The school counselor and/or lunch duty and recess duty staff are necessary when you can take a deep dive into the true unvarnished world of your students in school.

See how the students handle anger. Do they use profanity and name-calling as a means of targeting each other? Do they yell, scream, and threaten or do they play an active role in problem solving? Are they taking responsibility for their portion of an argument or do they, instead, blindly blame those around them? Do they let emotion and rage take over their angry rhetoric, or do they walk away and wait until cooler heads prevail?

PROVIDING STUDENTS WITH WHAT THEY NEED

Embedded in the curriculum of social skills within a school must be the discussion of anger and its parallel management. This should include

1. Conflict resolution skills curriculum that has outcome-based success.
2. Ways of dealing with bullying targets, perpetrators, and bystanders.
3. Means of decreasing stress (mediation, yoga, relaxation, anger management skills).
4. Support staff that one can turn to.
5. Parenting enrichment programs for parents to support a student's emotional well-being.
6. Role-playing to address issues that may arise regarding discord and anger.
7. Natural and logical consequences for behaviors that are sparked by anger that teach education versus simply discipline or punishment.
8. Methods to handle rejection and failure.
9. Attention to those who turn their anger internally and foster depressive traits and/or resentment.

NOTES

1. Daniel Goleman, *Emotional Intelligence: Why It Can Matter More Than IQ* (London: Bloomsbury, 1995).
2. Richard Knox, "The Teen Brain: It's Just Not Grown Up Yet," NPR, March 1, 2010, https://www.npr.org/templates/story/story.php?storyId=124119468.
3. Healthline Editorial Team, "Frontal Lobe," *Healthline*, March 2, 2015, https://www.healthline.com/human-body-maps/frontal-lobe/male.

Chapter Two

It's Not My Fault!

Encouraging Responsibility in Our Children

> In the final analysis, the one quality that all successful people have is the ability to take on responsibility. —Michael Korda

CHILD PROFILE

Ron is a nineteen-year-old whose favorite activity is playing video games. He does not have any friends to speak of aside from the multitude of those that he plays role-playing games with via his high-speed Internet connection or smartphone. He is slightly overweight from drinking too many sodas and eating the candy bars that are conveniently located in his mini-fridge in his room.

His room has the wrappers of various candies littered across it along with a mosaic of empty soda cans that are scattered along the deeply soiled carpet. When he wants, he comes down for dinner or makes himself a package of heavily salted noodles.

He interacts with his parents only when he wants or needs something. His mother and father have been bugging him to get a job, but he refuses to do so. He believes that it will take away from his time of scoring the highest rank in his video games. Ron also thinks, "Why should I?" Ron reclines back into his soft bed, puts on his new headphones, and pops in the next video game.

TEACHING A CHILD TO RIDE THE BIKE OF LIFE

Remember those days long ago, when you learned the childhood ritual of riding a bike? At first, your parent held the bicycle tightly and trotted alongside of you as you took your first wobbling, unsteady pedals. As you became more confident, they ran a little faster and eventually let you go. You pedaled, swaying along, uncertain at first, but building more and more confidence with each push of the pedal.

As your parents, they warned you of the dangers and made sure you wore your helmet and kneepads. They steadied and straightened your direction when you focused on looking at the pedals and drifted toward the danger of the impending curbs. Yes, you may have fallen, got the occasional scraped knee, and shed a few tears. However, your parents always dusted you off, cleaned your wounds, and put you back on the right path. In short, your parents carefully balanced your safety with your burgeoning desire for independence.

The scenario is a fitting analogy for parents and educators in developing a child's character. We must ration that careful blend of allowing freedom, security, and childhood growth. We must keep the youth going in the right direction on the road of life while giving them a subtle nudge from the harsh and unforgiving concrete curbs of the world.

THE ALL-INCLUSIVE VACATION

Picture an all-inclusive vacation; you are provided all the food you want, unlimited entertainment, Internet, and butler service. You do not have to lift a finger; it is all done for you. How much would you pay for this trip? A thousand dollars? Five thousand? What if I told you that you could have this service complimentary for the next eighteen-plus years?

Doesn't that sound like a virtual paradise?

This is often what occurs to many children that do not learn the habit of responsibility in their childhood. They are provided all the items they could ever need or want. In turn, they do not learn to develop motivation. Flash forward eighteen years and you have an "adult child," who is sitting playing video games, unemployed, and eating a bag of chips mindlessly. The parent is left questioning, why are they like this? The better question is, why would they not want/learn to be like this?

THE EPIDEMIC OF "HELICOPTERING"

A relatively recent epidemic of parenting styles has come to bear upon youth. It is known as "the helicoptering" parent, who hovers over a child's every move and need. They watch what the child does and what other peers do to their child and look for every opportunity to be needed by their son or daughter. This becomes an issue for child and parent alike in the following aspects:

1. As a child grows, the parental job is to pull back and let them mature and test their abilities for independence. This form of parenting does not provide this flexibility and staves off these opportunities.
2. It sends the message to the youngster "you can't do it" or "you can't be trusted to do it without help." The child begins to falsely believe they need someone else to ultimately be successful in any aspect of their life.
3. It creates anxiety for the parent, which then (verbally and nonverbally) is telegraphed to the child, creating the belief that the child must relieve the parent's anxiety (and vice versa).

Teaching responsibility is vital in a classroom setting. Students will take responsibility readily for an A; however, it may be a far more important lesson for them to take responsibility for what they did (or did not do) to honestly earn a lower grade. When they fail, do they blame others? Do they accuse the teacher? Or do they simply beat up on themselves or state they do not care?

Each of these is an important and topical conversation on responsibility and accepting it for the good as well as the bad. Taking responsibility for doing poorly shows a far more important social skill—maturity of taking responsibility.

In addition, teaching responsibility must be done in a clear, concise, and nonemotional manner school-wide. Why? Because in the real world if one does eighty miles per hour in a sixty-five-miles-per-hour zone in one part of the state, the law is relatively the same in another part. This means that you have some idea of consistency in terms of what should be your responsibility and potential consequences.

In schools, if I chew gum in Mrs. Smith's class, will I get the same consequence as if I chew gum in Mr. Jones's class? If I do not, it is much harder to learn responsibilities if these consequences vary from place to place in the same environment.

Taking the same scenario of the speeding car, if I get pulled over, is the police officer going to yell and scream and belabor me? Or is he going to use the calm and consistent voice of "License and registration please"? If you are a yeller as an educator, you will get far less taking responsibility due to fear of accepting blame (see below for more about this).

THE LANGUAGE OF MONEY AND EARNING

Often in parenting and education, the question is asked, do we need to provide incentives for a child to earn something? Isn't that, in effect, bribing a child to do a given task or activity?

Well, yes and no. A set of activities and chores should be expected in both the home and the classroom settings as a part of the role of being a part of a family or class. However, all of us are motivated by external and extrinsic motivations. If you do not believe this, think about why you go to work each day. It is, at least partially, due to the external reward of money and financial independence.

One of the issues that many parents as well as educators run into is that no reward seems to work for a particular child. They try "everything," and the child fails to step up to the plate and take responsibility for whatever necessary response is requested.

First off, if you want a child to foster responsibility and a decent work ethic, rewards and achievements must not be able to be received in any easier manner from some other source. Meaning, if I can get the low-lying fruit, why should I get a ladder to get those at the top? Therefore, responsibility is achieved only as a skill that must be tested and strengthened. In short, those in authority cannot allow an easier way around what a child must go through to strengthen their resolve. Therefore, avoid rewarding behaviors or inaction needlessly.

This is where the issue of allowance is so vital. A child does not learn the language of discipline, responsibility, and money if they can get their needs met in some other aspect. If they have to earn and save for something (whether through a reward system at school or at home), it is the main way to teach the language of money and savings. Case in point, a youth will be less apt to needlessly spend if they have to use their own money (or similar reward tokens).

THE MARSHMALLOW EXPERIMENT ON RESPONSIBILITY... NOT JUST FLUFF

In the 1970s, psychologist Walter Mischel at Stanford University conducted a series of experiments.[1] The concept of the test was simple, in that a child was offered a choice between one marshmallow now or two marshmallows if they waited until the researcher returned. The researcher would then leave the room for fifteen minutes, and when they returned (if the marshmallow was still intact), the child would receive two marshmallows as a reward for their patience in waiting. Why is this important?

The children of this research were followed into adulthood, and it was determined that those who were able to take the responsibility of disciplining themselves to wait for the two marshmallows had superior SAT scores, higher rates of educational success as adults, lower body mass indexes, and most other attributes necessary for success.[2] The bottom line: the younger a child can establish responsibility and self-discipline for themselves, the better a chance to sculpt success as an adult.

THE GOLDEN RULE OF RESPONSIBILITY

When we do anything that our child(ren)/students can do for themselves, we effectively disable them. The subtle, unwarranted message that we are giving them is "you are not capable of doing this on your own; you need help." This leads, in turn, to self-esteem problems and/or overreliance on others.

As Henry Ford once said, "If you think you can do a thing or think you can't do a thing, you're right." In terms of teaching or parenting if you tell a child directly or subtly they can't do something . . . "you're right." Take the case of a child trying their best to do a task and you do not like the way they are doing it and so you change it to the way *you* think is correct. The message is the child failed or is not good enough.

Ask the child to try the same, or similar, task later and they don't seem motivated or try at all. We now say, "See . . . they are unmotivated." From the child's perspective, they say, "Why bother? They are just going to change or correct it anyway." We have taught them the concept of "learned helplessness," a psychological term for, quite simply put, learning laziness or learning that throwing in the towel is more effective than trying.

DON'T SET UP A NO-WIN SITUATION

Let's suppose for a moment that your child or student spills a glass of milk across the table. Now, you ask the child, "Did you spill the milk?" Well, what are the child's choices in this matter?

1. If I admit that I spilled the milk, I get in trouble for spilling the milk based on what has occurred after mistakes of the past.
2. If I say I did not spill the milk, I possibly could get away with it and not get in any trouble.

The second choice might seem like the logical one if you are asking the child. Why? Because they have a 100 percent chance of getting in trouble with the first. If they indicate that they did not spill the milk, they may skirt past getting into trouble by not taking responsibility.

So how do we handle this issue? If you see a child do something wrong, confront them directly with the infraction. "You took the item when you were not supposed to and here is your consequence . . ." Do not give an opportunity for a child to try to skip out and lie or slough off responsibility in these cases. Approach the issue directly without "sugarcoating" or questioning something to which you know the response.

THE LOUDER THE VOICE, THE LESS THE RESPONSIBILITY

One certain way for a child not to muster responsibility is for an authority figure to scare them out of taking ownership for their actions. What does this mean?

Think about this for a moment. If you have to tell your boss, teacher, or significant other about a mistake you made and they are apt to explode and yell at you . . . do you really want to open that powder keg?

Most of us would say, "You know what? I am going to try to dance around the issue . . . rather than be yelled at or berated." So direct discussion of the situation is avoided or tabled to a later date (that may never arrive). The issues that are placed on the back burner by your children, unfortunately, grow and metastasize to larger unresolved issues as they transition into young adults.

Concerns start off innocuously—being afraid to tell Mom or Dad that we broke an item—and then morph as they get older to my friend wanted me to try marijuana. If as a child I am afraid to discuss the first with you, how on earth will I be prepared or willing to discuss the latter?

ALLOW THE STING OF CONSEQUENCES WHEN RESPONSIBILITY IS NOT TAKEN

Many times, we want to shield children from the bitter taste of taking responsibility for their actions. Parents often want to step in and tell the teacher, coach, or other authority figure why the youngster did not do what they were supposed to do. Or jump in and say, "That was not my child" (knowing full well it could have been) and then defend our child from the school, the club, or the world that they feel has so unjustly wronged them. When you defend wrong behavior from a child, you also stunt them from growing responsibility in a world that necessitates it for ultimate success and maturity.

In terms of fostering responsibility, adults must construct consequences that are "junior" or "miniature" versions of what the child can expect in the so-called real world of life. One may say, "In the real world that would never fly." True, but our goal is to teach children to "prepare" for that real world.

Here are just a few of the "real" world rules:

1. If a child is mean to other children, they will not want to be their friend.
2. If you steal or lie, you must confront the person (or persons) that you offended and it will not be fun.
3. If you procrastinate anything, you will have to make it up at some other time. Likely, that time will be at some period inconvenient to your social life, technology time, or watching your favorite television show(s).
4. If you spend it all, you will not have it when you want something bigger.
5. If you break it or mess it up, you must fix it or clean it.
6. Treating others the way you want to be treated is important, as is teaching others the way you want to be treated by them.
7. If you borrow, you must return it in the same condition.
8. If you agree to it, you should complete it.

Practical Application of These "Real" World Rules

1. If a child is nasty to other children, the community of children will behave much the same way as that of society in general. The child will be isolated and ostracized from their peers. This seems harsh and we may want to fight for our child to be accepted by their peers.

    However, if the aggressive child is to do so, they must first adapt their social skills accordingly. The response parallels later life: if you were to behave in an aggressive manner, your adult peers would shun you. This being said, we must make our children aware of what they need to change. Often, criticism is hidden, or made too subtle, by those who don't want to offend the youth. This leads to a child (and eventual adult) who "just never seems to get it."

2. If a child lies, they must be made to face the person/persons they lied to. As we discussed earlier, if you are untruthful, you must feel the discomfort of facing up to the person you deceived (no matter how uncomfortable). Additionally, if you steal, you must be encouraged to return the items along with some means of repayment: doing a good deed, such as community service (in place of some other desired activity) or giving an item or a portion of your allowance to a charitable cause (aka restitution).

3. Treating others the way you want to be treated is simple and self-explanatory. Yet it is infinitely difficult. However, it is a mirror as well that reflects equally back on the child accordingly. If they treat others in a certain way, they have to reflect a manner that is expectant for how they will be treated.

4. It is vital for children to understand the concept of money and being frugal with it. If you give them an allowance, they begin to understand that they have limited resources and are more inclined to be conservative with it. However, if they have an allowance and you still buy everything for them, they cannot possibly understand the language of financial responsibility in the confusion of such a mixed message.

5. If a child does break an item or makes a mess, it becomes their duty to fix it or clean it. An adult's job is only to support them in making this right. Being cushioned from the results (because we "feel bad for them") makes their actions someone else's problem.

Educational Application of Real World Rules

1. Clean up after yourself.
2. If you procrastinate doing work at school, it will be brought home and be done at a time that is inconvenient. Think of an adult example: if you are spending time in the faculty room or at the water cooler at work, then you will be doing that report or grading those papers versus going out for a drink with your friends or seeing that movie. Quite simply, the borrowed time is now "owed" and paid at another time inconvenient to you and your schedule.
3. If you borrow something from the library, a friend, or a teacher, it should be given back promptly and in the same condition it was found or you owe a new one.
4. If you do not do your work, it will be done at a time reciprocal to the time you wasted in school.
5. If you agree to do a group project or join an organization or a team, you have the responsibility to commitment for an equal part of what you are supposed to do or you receive the criticism of both peers and teachers and will be graded respectively.
6. You are responsible to ask questions and clarify work. It is not the teachers', peers', nor parents' responsibility.
7. You are responsible for being prepared and getting to class in a timely manner.

Are these commonsense? Yes. Are they always very commonly used? No. For some children, school is the only place that they have structure and are held to accountability. Do not take for granted that a youth knows what they are responsible for or how to take that role. This framework must be spelled out consistently and often for these are the basic tenets of the world they will inherit.

DON'T CONFUSE LACK OF RESPONSIBILITY FOR LACK OF ABILITY

Let us suppose that you wanted to be a rock star. If you were to be told that you would have a great musical contract of several million dollars, have a concert tour that will take you to all the exotic places you have always wanted to go, and you could bring any of your family all expenses paid, wouldn't you want do it?

That would, of course, be a great opportunity; however, if your voice sounds as scratchy as a wool sweater and your dance moves are as fluid as a robot, you are in serious trouble. It does not matter how much cash you are offered, how much the deal is sweetened; if you simply do not have the capabilities to do something, it may just be out of your scope of competence.

Often, in the world of parenting and education, we do the same thing, however. We believe that if we make the rewards large or attractive enough, this will energize the child/student toward motivation to complete the desired task. Sometimes, however, we are presenting a reward that due to a host of potential obstacles (physical, emotional, developmental, situational) a child is simply not capable of acquiring under any circumstance. If we keep pushing, we risk frustration and breaking the very will and esteem of the child. We must either tailor a more attainable goal and/or find a way of addressing the limitation in that particular domain first, before we can expect success later.

DEVELOP AN UNDERSTANDING OF DEVELOPMENT

Diapers and formula are expensive. Many a parent would like to have their child become potty trained and eating solid foods as soon as possible. Yet, as motivated as we are to do this, we firmly recognize this ability comes in time with a child's ensuing developmental capabilities.

So, when you ask a child to take responsibility for anything, the first question is simply, will they be able to do this at their current developmental stage? (See table 2.1 for a quick primer as to what a child is capable of generally being responsible for and when. Be aware that this chart is only a reference for typical development.) Children are quite variable and each meets their milestones in their own time frame accordingly.

DON'T FIGHT YOUR CHILD'S FIGHTS

Our children often get into minor conflicts and dramas with peers or siblings. Many times, our first response is to be reactive due to the emotional nature of children and our tendency to want to jump in and save the day.

The issue then becomes that a child does not have an opportunity to learn assertiveness skills. What they comprehend is that they are not capable of

Table 2.1. Estimated Age and Developmental/Social Skill Levels

Age	
0–1 Years	• Can be soothed by an adult they are familiar with. • Will generally accept and be quieted when picked up. • Smiles and laughs with positive social interactions. • Begins to acknowledge and recognize familiar faces. • Can start to display and comprehend basic emotional expressions in a clear manner. • May show discomfort when exposed to negative emotions and/or strangers. • Shows more comfort around familiar people and anxiety around strangers. • Can find ways to soothe themselves.
2–3 Years	• Is able to participate in small groups with other children. • Maintains eye contact with others. • Is not overly anxious when exploring new situations and can transition from one scenario to another. • Likes to play with various toys and objects. • Will sit and look at a book. • Usually happy and/or able to soothe themselves. • Is developing an established and reliable sleeping schedule. • Expresses sadness when hurt. • Will play near (but not always with) peers.
3–5 Years	• Comprehends what is positive versus negative behaviors. • Begins to have peers that they befriend. • Imitates behaviors of adults. • Is developing skills of empathy. • Likes to play and utilize imagination skills.
5–8 Years	• Understands concept of playing, sharing, and taking of turns with peers. • Begins to comprehend different feelings. • Starts to realize the link of cause and effect/consequences of actions. • Can express their feelings in words. • Is capable of empathizing in correspondence to others. • Is able to separate fantasy versus reality. • Understands and tells/understands basic humor. • Comprehends and utilizes imagination.

8–10 Years	• Prefers playing with others versus independently. • Begins development of longer-lasting friendships. • Becomes more independent and rule oriented. • Is increasingly concerned with adult and peer approval. • May become increasingly moody/dramatic. • Starts to recognize their own mood changes and expression. • Grows into a more competitive individual and wants to participate in organized competitive activities. • Starts to understand and take responsibility for actions and behaviors. • Can assert a particular point of view and argument.
11–13 Years	• Increasingly more proficient at using assertiveness skills. • Cares more about peer pressure, material items, clothing, etc. • Continues to refine empathy skills. • Develops the understanding that there are consequences to their actions. • Recognizes cause and effect. • Is better able to handle negative emotions. • Has the ability to be more persistent; develops leadership and community-based skills. • Sees fairness as a "black and white" concept. • Realizes character education traits and values.
14–18 Years	• Begins to be aware of what traits are their strengths and weaknesses. • Starts to distance from parents. • Increases social circles. • Develops some discord and separation from parents and requests independence. • Sees friends as more important. • Begins to experience dating as a vital lifestyle element. • Experiences a maturing ability to make decisions.

Sources: Partially adapted from "Important Milestones: Your Child by Three Years," Centers for Disease Control and Prevention, https://www.cdc.gov/ncbddd/actearly/milestones/milestones-3yr.html; "Social and Emotional Development in School-Age Children," *AboutKidsHealth*, http://www.aboutkidshealth.ca/En/HealthAZ/DevelopmentalStages/SchoolAgeChildren/Pages/Social-and-Emotional-Development.aspx; "Child Development," Centers for Disease Control and Prevention, https://www.cdc.gov/ncbddd/childdevelopment/index.html.

standing up for themselves and/or are in need of constant rescuing. This, in turn, damages their self-esteem and ability to take responsibility for their actions and emotions. Further, it also does not allow them to begin to foster a repertoire of conflict resolution skills necessary for them to carry throughout their lives. In short, "don't do for them what they are capable of handling themselves."

RESPONSIBILITY BEGINS WITH "U"

Responsibility is not just a social trait necessary for children. Just watching the television or surfing the web will provide a plethora of adults behaving badly and then not taking any credit or responsibility for the carnage left in their wake. Leaders, athletes, actors . . . the list goes on and on of adults who shun taking accountability and point a finger at others.

Similarly, when we become angered at a situation or the general unfairness of life, we tend to point our finger of responsibility at those all around us. Remember, however, our next generation in earshot is learning much more by what you do than what you say.

WHAT IS WITHIN THE CHILDHOOD TOOLBOX OF RESPONSIBILITY?

If a child is going to learn responsibility, then we must develop the capacity for children to use skills that are necessary to do so. Children have only a limited scope of influence and power in the adult world. However, in preparing them for the world, we must teach them the skills necessary to survive as well as thrive.

A child cannot take responsibility for their actions if they do not know what components are within their scope of abilities to utilize. So let us take a look at what topics we should be teaching children to exercise their capabilities in.

SINCERE APOLOGIES

When a child has done wrong, they should be obligated to learn and give a sincere apology. This is not the same as a child who does a "knee-jerk" apology in which they just reflexively apologize for everything that they do, hence encouraging apologies that are empty and meaningless.

However, it also means (as discussed earlier) that we should find a way of restitution for the wrong expeditiously. At times, we want to punish and teach a child "who is boss." This does nothing to serve the primary task, which is to teach discipline and a life lesson. If you cannot find how the advice you are teaching is analogous to a life lesson, then it may just be that you are harboring a punishment or empty threat.

LEARN HOW TO EXPRESS FEELINGS IN AN ASSERTIVE MANNER AND TAKE RESPONSIBILITY FOR YOUR EMOTIONS

- When a child is young and has limited ability to use words and control emotions, they will tantrum and leave parents and adults scrambling to play a game of charades trying to find what will appease them. However, as a child becomes older, they should be taught to state what they are feeling, why they feel that way, and how to solve the problem accordingly.
- It is okay for a child to have a particular feeling; however, it is not the job of those around the youth to guess what they are feeling and predict what they need to remedy the issue. We all know adults like this. They give us the "silent treatment" and we are left to guess what is bothering them and what it was that offended them. For all of us, this is an ineffective means of relationship building. Imagine walking into your boss and trying this strategy?

    We must teach our children, therefore, responsibility for their emotions and actions, specifically that they are allowed to feel the range of emotions (positive and negative) and express them in a useful manner. Nevertheless, if they want an adult to assist with handling a particular issue, they must (a) address what is bothering them and (b) give some potential thoughts on how to fix the situation.

- This applies to problem solving as well. Children must learn to take responsibility for themselves in conflict. They have to become skilled at how to address a problem without resorting to hitting (aggression) or being a "doormat" (passivity). Therefore, they can try and develop productive solutions when they have discord with peers or siblings. As stated earlier, as adults we must be willing and able to allow them to stretch their wings of conflict resolution by trying out various means to address problems independently. Not to mention, children tend to have conflict with a peer one day and are best friends the next moment without adult interference.

    A word of caution, however: we must step in to stop true physical aggression. In addition, there is sometimes a tendency toward suggesting "playground rules" to youth. That is, "if he hits you, you hit him back." The difficulty with that is both youngsters could get hurt. Additionally, in the adult world, both persons could end up very hurt (especially if one pulls a weapon) or both risk criminal/civil charges.

KNOW WHAT CHILDREN CAN HANDLE AND WHAT THEY CAN'T (OR SHOULDN'T)

If we spend all of our day taking care of the multitude of relatively trivial issues our children encounter, we waste a great deal of our time in empty conflicts and an endless run on the drama treadmill of childhood angst and anxiety.

Therefore, if we are going to teach kids responsibility we must first allow them to organize whose responsibility is that of an adult and what is the role of the child. Let us look at the precarious road that happens if we saddle children with "adult-like" responsibilities.

Children think they want to be handed the role of responsibility because with it comes control that they have such a desperate lack of in an adult-oriented world. Oftentimes, parents make the cardinal error of allowing children to be exposed to the so-called adult world of issues like divorce, bills, mortgages, and the like. Doing so creates adult-like anxiety for children who have no means of controlling these issues within the myopic scope of control of youth.

PLAY WASTEPAPER BASKETBALL

Our next generation must understand and have a strategy for separation between what is within their control and what should best be deferred into the capable hands of adults.

Remember, children communicate and work in the world of play. Along this vein, we will utilize play to teach what is the role of each party (adult and child) in various dimensions of responsibility.

Therefore, let us suppose we have two trash cans—one is for the job of adults and the second the role of the child. We can play a game now (either actually playing this game or imagining doing so).

Those items that go into the first "can" are those issues that we do not want children to even attempt to take responsibility for handling. These include scenarios such as

"The Adult Can"

1. Anyone that tells them to keep secrets from their parents (with the exception of surprise parties/gifts of course).

2. Issues of harassment, intimidation, or bullying.
3. Any time they are "dared" to do anything.
4. Issues in which they, a sibling, or a peer could potentially be hurt.
5. When they are asked to do something or try something, they are not comfortable with doing.
6. Any issue that can remotely cause emotional or physical injury.
7. Adult issues of bills, marriage, and work status.

"The Child Can"

1. Issues of usual sibling or peer conflict (that are not physical).
2. Homework or activities that they should be capable of but have not given themselves a reasonable opportunity to attempt.
3. Waiting patiently to do something that they are eager to do.
4. Finding an activity to entertain themselves versus asking an adult to assist them due to "boredom."

"Children Should Toss into the Adult Can"

1. Any, and all, matters in which your peer, or anyone else, has the potential for (or is engaged in) dangerous activities.
2. Scenarios in which anyone suggests keeping something secretive from parents.
3. Concerns in which you have "butterflies in your stomach" and do not know why.
4. Problems that involve discussions related to harassment, intimidation, or bullying.
5. Suggestions in which a peer/peers try to dare you to do something or exert negative peer pressure/influence.
6. Any concern that you are not certain if you should (or could) handle the topic in an appropriate fashion.

Note: It must be made very clear to youth that adults do not want children to handle issues for which youngsters are unequipped or not emotionally or mentally ready to tackle. Therefore, when the topics are adult oriented or dangerous, they must be deferred to adults quickly and always.

EDUCATIONAL APPLICATION

The role of responsibility is never so glaringly clear as that of a student's responsibility within a school setting. For many children, this is the very first experience in having to take ownership for what they do, experiencing failure or disappointment, and learning to navigate with others who vie for the attention of the teacher, school sports, or clubs.

Therefore, this is the natural place that responsibility should be taught and discussed. To foster an environment of responsibility, the following are useful within the public school arena:

1. Allow for failure: Oftentimes, parents are afraid of their children failing. Allowing for failure and disappointment may sometimes be the natural consequence a child needs in order to recognize that they are responsible for their school work and attendance.
2. Don't belabor mistakes: When a teacher overly harps on mistakes, students may be less willing to step to the plate and accept their role. Therefore, less discussion and not being overly reactive allows the pupil to feel comfortable to come into the light of acceptance for what they have done.
3. Encourage positive responsibility: We are all tuned to remember the negative more than the positive. Not certain of this? Remember the most negative thing ever said to you. It is much easier to recall than the kindest words ever uttered in your presence. Therefore, be certain to celebrate and feed the accomplishments of the children in your school so they bask in the light of positive responsibility.
4. Create responsibility and tasks: Giving students "chores and tasks" in class and in the school allows them to know that they have a function in the school. Adults run everything in their lives and yet school is a student-centered world . . . let them know this.
5. Take responsibility for your own mistakes: Nothing is more disheartening to a student than to see an authority figure not take responsibility for their own emotions or mistakes. If you make a mistake or become emotional, immediately accept full charge for it.
6. Have parents involved: Parents are the greatest model of responsibility for a child; invite them to participate in school and in their child's learning.

NOTES

1. Walter Mischel, Robert Zeiss, and Antonette Zeiss, "Internal-External Control and Persistence: Validation and Implications of the Stanford Preschool Internal-External Scale," *Journal of Personality and Social Psychology* 29 , no. 2: 265–78.

2. Ibid.

Chapter Three

There Is a Big World Out There

Practical Social Skills

Play gives children a chance to practice what they are learning. —Fred Rogers

CHILD PROFILE

Beth is a thirteen-year-old middle school student. She loves gardening and talks about flowers, seeds, weeds, and planting all the time. It is a bit of an obsession. It is her hope to work in a greenhouse or as a florist when she gets older.

Beth has another goal; she wants friendships desperately. When she comes up to other children in school, she excitedly tells them about her garden and her vegetables and describes all of the trees that dot the landscape of her school.

The other girls tell her to "get out of their personal space" and continue to play and gossip noisily as a few snicker at Beth. With tears in her eyes, Beth walks away with her head hung low in disappointment.

THE "PLAYER PIANO" MANNER OF "TEACHING" SOCIAL SKILLS

When I was a child, our family had a player piano. We would carefully place the yellowing rolls on the top of the gears. As the rolls spun around, the keys would press down in perfect harmony and sequence as though a ghostly expert pianist had taken a seat at our piano. Oftentimes, my sister or I would pretend to play the piano. We became quite proficient at "pretending" to be virtuosos.

We can make a parallel with "teaching" or "learning" social skills. Many of the abilities we try to teach can be "played" back to us in rigid black and white tones. Yet the world of social skills has so many shades of gray that when a child tries to apply them in the real world, it comes across as "canned, phony, or inauthentic." Frequently, this artificial interactive style is a turnoff for potential friendships. Peers seem to have a keen, tacit knowledge that something seems off or not genuine in the interaction and thus back away.

As a teacher (or school counselor), therefore, this is the time to be "in earshot" of the children as they interact. Are they talking about appropriate subjects? Do they allow for back and forth dialogue? Do they only talk about themselves or ask questions? Here is the time for educators to listen and perform the role of life coach, in a sense, offering suggestions and telling them to "get back out there" to the field of peer interaction.

THE DANGER OF STARVING SOCIAL SKILLS

There is often an unintended consequence to children who do not have an opportunity to exercise their social skills muscles. Children who do not have these needs met will try to find some alternative way to fulfill this desire, but not generally in the most appropriate venues. Children, like us all, will seek a means to get their needs met in some alternative manner.

Let us imagine that your child does not have any play dates, has no siblings, and/or has limited social opportunities. They will seek to satisfy this craving at less appropriate times and junctures. For instance, if a child's sole peer outlet is in school, they will utilize this venue to satisfy their needs. It does not matter if the teacher stands on their head; if the motivation the youth has for peer interaction is greater than learning, they will follow that road. If the youngster believes that the need for socializing is of greater reinforcement to them personally, they will seek that every time. It is not that they do not want the positive reinforcement of the adult; it is just the adulation and laughter with those their own age is simply a more important reward.

Rewards, consequences, and any other motivators tried are moot and inconsequential in this case. The child is like a virtual "kid in a candy store" seeking the greater reward of any kind of immediate peer social interaction versus the lower reinforcement of the teacher's or any other adult figures' verbal praise.

CHILDREN THAT ONLY UNDERSTAND THE LANGUAGE OF "ADULT"

Case in point, regarding social skills: let us suppose a child comes to school who is an only child. Predominantly, by logic, they are perpetually around adults. What they hear is adult talk: adult humor, adult sarcasm, and adult concerns. When they say something that sounds grown-up for their age, it is reinforced with a parent chuckle and "Oh . . . isn't that cute?"

Now, picture that same child arriving at school for their first day among a gaggle of kindergarteners. They try to engage their peers with those existing "adult-like" social skills. The children do not understand this method of conversation. Conversely, that child looks at their fellow five-year-olds discussing topics common to five-year-olds and thinks to themselves, "Why are these kids acting like a bunch of five-year-olds?" This will continue year after year until the peers' maturity levels reach that of the child's more "adult-like" perceptions and engagement with others.

Oddly, it will take those same adults to teach the youth how to be able to interact among their peers in an age-appropriate manner. It is as if a child such as this one, must be taught a language that is native and natural to their peer group.

THE COMPETENT FLIGHT SIMULATOR PILOT

If you were to board a plane and the pilot were to tell you they logged ten thousand hours on a flight simulator but this was their first actual flight, would you trust their skills? My guess would be a resounding no.

Yet we try a parallel strategy when we tell a child to practice "simulated" social skills solely through interaction with adults (teachers, therapists, etc.) and then tell them to go out and use these rehearsed skills in the real world. The sole use of this technique is frequently doomed for failure when practice comes to application.

PROVIDE "ON THE JOB TRAINING"

If children are going to be socially competent, they must practice this ability like any other of a bevy of comparable skills. Today, parents are drowning in the carpools of taking children to a host of classes from dance to football, music to equestrian, karate to boxing. These activities are helpful provided they do not create an overwhelming source of anxiety for child and parent alike.

Despite the critical nature of these organized activities, however, the only way for a child to succeed in socialization is through the practice of being social with other children. Socializing is like exercising to develop muscles or stamina to run a marathon. One must strengthen their social skills and need to specifically practice, fail, and retune their technique for ultimate success.

Therefore, planned play dates provide the "on the job" training in doing so. It is through these small-group or one-to-one interactions that a child can experiment as to what works and what does not when conversing with peers. A parent or teacher that remains in earshot can give immediate feedback regarding interacting in "real time" and applicable to the situation at hand. These opportunities cannot be replaced by rigidly organized activities that are closely adult monitored and offer little room for social experimentation.

Often, we are too quick to pull a child away from what we perceive as social failure. However, if we make the analogy to one of a child doing a jigsaw puzzle, we would not pull that same child away when they clumsily try and shuffle pieces back and forth, twist and turn them. We would sit back patiently and wait for that all important "uh huh" moment when the puzzle pieces finally are fit together. So too with social skills. They take time, failure, readjustment, and then eventual success.

ALL HANDS ON DECK WITH SOCIAL SKILLS

Development of a team approach toward social skills coaches is vital in order for any social skills program or intervention to work. The "team" should all be on the same page. That means a skill (such as conversation starting) must have the buy-in of teachers, counselors, supervisors, and coaches for consistency and delivery of a parallel message.

The difficulty for children with application of social skills is that it is not "a simple one size fits all" approach. When a child is in varied situations, a rote script that they may utilize in one social opportunity may not be appropriate or useful in another. When a youth has only an experience of how to apply a single or limited techniques in a situation, they may try to jam themselves into other scenarios using the same imperfect social skills that are ineffective or don't quite fit into the new problem. When it fails, if they do not have other tools, they just will try harder with greater emotion and frustration to make the restrictive skill set work. This only leads to a repetitive cycle of increased resistance by peers and eventual social isolation.

It is necessary, therefore, that this child has that crew of adults who are at the ready to help them shift the proverbial gears of their social skills for each idiosyncratic situation when they become stuck in the inevitable social mud of life. This must take place with constant, consistent, and prompt reactions during times when social skill education is at its most pivotal.

When are these times specifically? Quite simply, the venues where adults are typically least involved: namely, at the playground, recess, lunch, play dates, and so on. Having adults present at these vital junctures to observe and play the role of life coach can help to smoothly shift through the gears of social life existence.

One may say, "That is not realistic. Who has time for all of these adults to be involved in one child's day?" A parallel to consider is that social skills are a lot, again, like riding a bike. It only takes a quick redirect and reminder to keep the bike up, balanced, and moving straight ahead (not constant and intensive interventions). Less is more, and a quick reminder is often all it takes to get the youth back on track socially.

TECHNOLOGY IS THE NEW WORLD OF SOCIALIZATION

Social media is everywhere and so it can be a spoke in the wheel of teaching social skills. If a child does not learn how to be a citizen of the digital world as well as the "brick and mortar" one, then there is a real possibility that they will be left in the dust of many socialization opportunities.

According to Dr. Carrie Barron, in a 2015 article entitled "How Technical Devices Influence Children's Brains," "The fast pace of online activity is not only altering the way young people's brains process information, but such activity is also physically changing their brains. The overuse of online activity is reconfiguring children's brains and forcing the field of education to adjust accordingly."[1]

Perhaps you may not believe that brains can actually be rewired by technology; however, I ask you this, can you remember the phone numbers of five of your friends? Alternatively, when was the last time you followed someone's directions to a location or read a map (not GPS)? It is now a rarity for anyone to be able to do these basic tasks that previously were a part of most people's regular repertoire.

Without a doubt, technology is (by far) the favorite medium for children to communicate with each other. Watch a group of teenage girls walking and you will see them shoulder to shoulder texting each other with no attempt at actual verbal communication.

As a result, a child's social skills training must include mastery in such areas as social media etiquette, how to handle cyberbullying, the dangers of texting pictures, and the potential of engaging with individuals whom one does not know (more on this later).

DOES YOUR CHILD WANT TO SOCIALIZE?

This is a difficult reality to sometimes swallow; however, our children all exist on a continuum of socialization between introversion and extroversion. Our society, falsely, believes that extroverted people are always best adjusted to the world around them. It should be noted many other cultures find introversion a far more respectful demeanor than that of the United States (which leans to the converse).

In truth, some children simply enjoy alone time and find it draining and unsatisfying to be in the constant presence of other children. For others, they are used to being around adults. Grown-ups are simply more predictable and more likely to accept, listen, and give them the things they want. After all, how many times have you seen a child fight with an adult about the game they are going to play or the toy that they want?

If a child is more introverted, they also tend to be more introspective and can watch the world around them from a distance. In turn, these kids develop understanding, in a pensive fashion, of how relationships work as opposed to those who are always speaking (versus listening). Of course, those who are more reserved should be able to muster the social skills at the times that such talents are required for ultimate success in a world that does require social interaction. That being said, however, it just may not be a child's primary motivation to have to exercise those attributes in a constant fashion with others around them unless necessary.

How do we know then if an introverted child is deficient and in need of bolstered social skills? If they are happy and feel satisfied with their current academic, social, and behavioral aspects of their lives and it is not an obstacle to others . . . what is the harm of allowing them this comfort? Further, if the major barriers of social skills do not adversely affect their behavior, health, academics, vocation, or the rights of others, then it may not need to come to the immediate forefront of concern. We must ask, whose issue is this—ours or theirs?

NOT ALL CHILDREN CONSIDER "PLAY" TO BE THE SAME ACTIVITY

We often assume that socialization equals activity. If a child is outside or on the playground, they should be physically active. As obesity levels have risen to astronomical degrees, there is no doubt that appropriate exercise is a vital and necessary activity.

Unfortunately, it is not that simple. Some children prefer being engaged in more introverted activities such as reading or playing a board game. Forcing them to engage in activities far outside their social comfort zone creates the issue of socializing as well as engaging in activities that they do not inherently want to do. Again, this is not downplaying the importance of physical activity. It is just to realize that the stereotype of "kids running around playing" is not the inherent pastime that all youth prefer.

FIND SIMILAR INTERESTS

According to relational psychology, two of the best ways to determine the success of a budding friendship are proximity (how close one person is to another and how often) and similar interests (hobbies, subjects, etc.).[2]

Therefore, to feed a potential successful friendship is to place a child in close proximity to a peer(s) who has/have similar interests. This will likely plant the relationship in the most fertile soil for a friendship to potentially bloom.

The following are the necessary elements for the potentially successful incubation of social interactional success:

- organized activity that allows time for free socialization,

- interaction that is based on the specific and mutually shared interests of those involved,
- proximity of peers to each other to facilitate social activity outside the organized activity,
- parental involvement to organize dates and times for the children to get together as a follow-up to the organized activity.

Of course, the converse is true. If you want a child to not have a relationship with another child who is a bad influence, significantly limit the time and contact they have and you will prune out that relationship from your child's social tree.

CHILDREN THAT NO LONGER WANT TO PARTICIPATE IN A DESIGNATED SOCIAL ACTIVITY

Many of our children's social calendars are so chock full of events that they would make any event planner's datebook buckle under the strain. Dance, equestrian, football, baseball, soccer, chess, and a host of other activities leave parent and child alike stressed. It may make one strongly consider painting the family minivan taxicab yellow and donning a chauffeur's cap on a semipermanent basis.

Mothers and fathers often then run into the very real question of what to do if/when my child wants to abandon an activity. The issue becomes, if I let them quit, will they inherently absorb that quitting is okay?

This point is a very valid question. In doing so, one must think of the following points:

- Is this an activity that the child wants to do or the parent "requires" them to do?
- How long have they been doing this activity and are they successful?
- Are they involved in other recreation or hobbies?
- If they leave this pursuit, what are they going to replace that gap of time with accordingly?
- Does the child have free, unstructured time (a necessary component for any of our mental health)?
- Does the child want to quit the activity, or are they having anticipation anxiety about a particular event that is coming up?

- What is the child's interpretation of quitting the activity? ("I decided to focus on other activities" versus "I can't do it. . . . I am a loser. . . . I quit.")

It is important that, if a child is reaching a particular milestone (a big game or a test) in this hobby, they try to attempt to complete that before they decide to simply exit and throw in the towel. Why? Because others may be counting on them, they have prepared for the task at hand, and if they do not try, they will receive the not-so-subtle message that when you are anxious or unsure simply quit and you will never fail (nor succeed). In doing so, the mountain of anticipation at the next big hurdle will be that much larger.

WATCH FOR THE DEFEATING WORDS IN SOCIAL SKILLS

Sometimes children will "psyche" themselves out before they even initiate the process of socializing. It is far easier to not try than risk the pain and disappointment of outright failure.

Watch for these self-defeating obstacles to friendships:

- "All or nothing thinking": Children sometimes think they must be totally successful or they will totally fail at socializing. In reality, social skills are not an either/or proposition. Due to the concrete nature and lack of abstract thinking, however, some youngsters think either they have to be best friends or they are not truly friends with others. In reality, we have relationships across the spectrum from stranger to acquaintance to friend. The harsh reality to be learned is you cannot be friends with everyone, nor will each child you meet want to be your friend.
- "Not seeing the gray areas": Socializing is, again, a gray area activity. That is, it is rarely something that can be defined by the simple constructs of "right" or "wrong." This is difficult for children who are very concrete (especially children with a potential developmental disability). Youth seek to find a black or white response to most issues. Therefore, we must help children to see the gray shades between what they believe to be "right or wrong/fair or unfair/good or bad."

A prime example of this mode of childhood thinking occurs in the educational setting. For example, a child will point out to a substitute teacher the "correct way" the traditional teacher does things. They see the regular teacher's routine as the right and only means possible. It does not occur to them that there are a variable number of alternate means of doing the same thing. Therefore, as adults it is important that we show them a number of alternate ways to look at the same experience, in short, helping them to see that socialization is not an "either/or" situation but something that can be addressed in any number of possible ways. It is through brainstorming with an adult that they can develop and garner new methods.

- Not every social situation (nor person) is the same: Some children are more persistent in attempting to socialize, while other youth are more apt to give up quickly. A child may use a limited one or two attempts at socializing and then determine that "everyone" or "no one" will accept their means of socializing with them. In short, encouraging a child to not generalize one or two situations to an entire life skill is of vital importance as they are basing a broad response on very limited information.
- When a child is wrong: Children, like adults, sometimes make assumptions based on little, or false, evidence about the actual situation. For instance, let us suppose that a child sees a peer walking down the hallway and greets them with a simple but barely audible "hello." The peer that they attempted to engage walks by them without any acknowledgment of their greeting. The child who evoked the greeting may now surmise the following:

- "I said something that hurt their feelings."
- "They don't like me and so they ignored me."
- "They hate me!"
- "They are rude and I am never talking to them again."

There are, however, of course, several alternative logical means of looking at this scenario that a child will tend to overlook. Yet these are just as viable possibilities that are far less devastating and disruptive to their socialization. For instance,

- "Perhaps they did not hear me."
- "Maybe they have headphones in their ears and can't hear."
- "Maybe they were thinking about something else."
- "Maybe I spoke too quietly or it was too loud in the hallway for them to hear."

It is in these ways the child starts arguing with the internal dialogue in their head that discourages them from believing in their social skills abil-

ities. Thus, such dialogue prevents degrading their self-confidence and esteem further.
- "It is not all about them": Children (and most adults) tend to see any situation that occurs as, what is my role in this outcome or in its initiation? Questions of "Why did they do this to me?" lead down a long road of feeling sorry for yourself and believing that you are a perpetual victim. In reality, many social issues do not occur because someone sought *to do* something to you; rather, it was because you were simply *not thought of* by another youth who was also egocentric in their own right. This allows the youngster to think of another hypothesis outside their own narrow beliefs of self-centered motivations and fears.
- Blaming others does not help you: When we make mistakes, all of us have a tendency to blame others. Quite simply, it is easier to cushion our own fragile ego by saying that we did not do or are not responsible for something. Children tend to blame peers for not socializing or, alternatively, they will skew a situation so it makes them appear to be a victim. As a direct consequence, they have "no fault" for a relationship or situation not working out in the social arena. This does not help because it limits the child's own inherent ability to dissect the communications and observe what they might have done differently.

Let us look at an alternative example: suppose a parent is making a child dinner and starts with the innocuous question of "What do you want for dinner?" The parent goes through the long litany of potential foods. The child then tells the parent, "I don't want this or that" and then blames the parent for making the wrong meal and for causing them to be disappointed. The child falsely believes that telling someone what you *do not* want is productive communication for telling what *you do* want or need.

A child must learn that emotional regulation and changes come from learning versus blaming others for what went wrong or what they did. In short, social skills develop from first recognizing the need to change and then doing so.

TOO CLOSE FOR COMFORT

When our children are preschool and kindergarten age, they may not have a good awareness of personal space around them. When they sit on the carpet or gather in groups, they tend to bang together like a rack of pool balls.

However, this tends to create hostility among peers and the reaction that is received by the peers can be equally harsh. Simultaneously, it is frustrating and confusing for the child who does not understand the reaction that they receive due to a lack of spatial awareness.

Role-playing for our children on an asphalt driveway can be useful: draw concentric circles in chalk (with your child in the middle) and discuss who should be in which circle(s), defining strangers, friends, family, and self. Review, when an imagined child or adult is too close to you or someone else, how that may make the child or the other person feel. This type of direct criticism and suggestion is necessary for a child to understand consistently and immediately. That being said, often others either react or do not provide this much-needed information in a timely fashion for this skill to be learned.

THE GAMES KIDS PLAY

Children's games have rules. We are not talking about the specific, concrete rules for a game like tag. Rather, we are talking about the subtle and tacit guidelines that children follow as their own social society out of the view of adults.

Rule 1: Games Have a Natural Starting and Ending Point

Typically, if children are in the middle of a game or activity, they must finish this role before they allow another peer or peers into the group. This means that if a child attempts to "jam" themselves into an activity in the middle or at the wrong time, they are likely to be rejected.

Further, a child with lessened social skill abilities will continue to "bang their head" against the proverbial wall of trying to enter the respective activity with these children without much success, thus decreasing their self-esteem because they believe their peer group as a whole is rejecting them. Most never think of the alternative coping strategy of seeking out other children or activities outside the immediate peer circle unless it is specifically pointed out to them.

Rule 2: Look for the Wallflowers

Teaching a child to scan the environment when initially rejected by the first peer group for acceptance by another will greatly increase the likelihood that a secondary group of peers will welcome them.

Assisting your child with practice then in assessing when an activity will be over when they want to join a group is immensely useful. This can be helpful at a playground, dance, or other peer/social event.

Rule 3: Teach Your Child a "Pick-Up" Line for Conversation

Now, I do not suggest a cheesy line that would be used for dating. What I mean is we all have statements and questions that we use to engage acquaintances around us. Teaching a child to ask a question, give a compliment, or state something they have in common is the first step to developing deeper conversations. In short, the more open-ended questions a child has in a rehearsed script in their back pocket the better.

Open-ended questions include

1. What is your favorite video game? Why?
2. What is your favorite board game? Why?
3. How do you do that (whatever activity)? Can you show me?
4. Whom do you play with? Can I play? What are the rules in this game?
5. What is the homework? Do you find it easy or hard?

Rule 4: A Novel Skill or Item Can Be a Novel Way of Drawing In Others

If your child has some item or skill that their peers do not have or draws their curiosity, this can often be an unusual icebreaker yet very effective. Examples of this include

- an unusual ability, such as being able to draw;
- learning and being able to do a magic trick in front of a crowd of peers;
- having a new toy or video game (last option).

These opportunities generate curiosity among the child's peer group, and other children are further drawn to the child like moths to a flame. Generating a quick flurry of interest and popularity can be utilized to garner and then harness friendships.

Rule 5: Most Other Kids Stay Away from the "Know-It-All," "Boss," or "Rule Keeper"

Often, these are roles children with social skills deficits may try to occupy as they begin to feel more comfortable and try to find a place in the social and conversational arena. Be on the lookout for this and squelch it as soon as you can, as it can grow into a socialization obstacle and perhaps lead to further rejection/isolation.

EDUCATIONAL APPLICATION

Generally, school is the one place that youth congregate together. It represents a slice of the socioeconomic, cultural, and racial makeup of each faction of a community. This makes it the best petri dish from which our pupils can formulate the necessary social skills to build a scaffolding necessary for adult life.

To develop a good social skills program within a school system, we must consider the following:

- Be where you are needed most: The times that social skills are most tested and the student's integrity is most needed occur where teachers are least present: lunch, recess, locker rooms, bathrooms. Obviously we cannot be in some of these locations (bathrooms and locker rooms); however, where we can be present is where we need to listen in earshot and coach our students along to make good decisions socially.
- Encourage organized activities and team building among all stakeholders: The first necessary component for socialization is the time to do so. Organized activities and team building allow students to work together toward common philanthropic or other goals. It should be noted that this occurs from "the top down," so a school faculty that work as a team models for a pupil community to do so as well.
- Role model social skills within the classrooms: It should not be assumed that all children know and can employ social skills. Think again of that child that was an only child and solely interacted with adults. When they arrive in school, how are they supposed to learn how to interact with those twenty years younger than anyone that they talked with previously? Lessons should include from the outset socialization, greetings, and conflict resolution skills.

- Encourage problem solving: Especially young children like to involve the teacher in minor squabbles and issues. Encouraging them to take care of the minor issues and offering potential solutions will allow negotiation skills necessary for a child to thrive and prosper.
- Encourage raising one's hand as a social skill: Have you ever met people that talk over you or don't let you get a word in edgewise? When a child blurts out an answer, that is the junior equivalent. Therefore, stressing that you must wait to be called on and, if the pupil has trouble remembering this, encouraging that they have to put their finger on their lips to keep themselves quiet every time they raise their hand can assist in this manner.
- Encourage kindness: The most vital rule may also be the simplest. Be kind in the words you say, with your hands as well as your feet, and follow the "golden rule." Touting this often and always, as well as trying to be "the best me that I can be" versus competing, can go a long way toward practical social skills.

DEVELOPING A SOCIAL SKILLS CURRICULUM

For a district to undertake a social skills curriculum, it is important that we look not just in one class, one grade, or one school. Rather, social skills must be a program that can be carried and adjusted in its development and expectations throughout a student's growth and development. See the appendix for examples.

NOTES

1. Carrie Barron, "How Technical Devices Influence Children's Brains," *Psychology Today*, May 18, 2015, https://www.psychologytoday.com/blog/the-creativity-cure/201505/how-technical-devices-influence-childrens-brains.

2. Gretchen Rubin, "8 Tips for Making Friends," *Psychology Today*, September 8, 2011, https://www.psychologytoday.com/blog/the-happiness-project/201109/8-tips-making-friends.

Chapter Four

A Walk in Someone Else's Shoes

Helping to Develop Compassion and Empathy

Empathy grows as we learn. —Alice Miller

CHILD PROFILE

Sharon is an eighteen-year-old who is in an inclusion class at her local public high school. She often is a "know-it-all," sticking her nose into others' business and giving advice with little to no information. She can often be deemed a "bully" as well because she indicates she simply "does not care what other people think."

She has been known to make others cry by embarrassing or laughing at them. She enjoys spreading rumors or teasing students if it will mean that her name will get around school. She does not care if her popularity is at the expense of others; she simply wants to be popular (good, bad, or indifferent).

WHY IS EMPATHY SUCH A DIFFICULT SKILL FOR CHILDREN?

"Kids can be cruel." That is a time-tested mantra that is often uttered by adults in relation to how children treat each other. If you remember as a child being picked last or being teased or bullied, you may be quick to affirm that this is indeed the case.

Children are blatantly honest and curious. First, as younger concrete thinkers, they are taught (hopefully) not to lie. Hence they often will give the unvarnished, unfiltered truth of how they see things. If the person beside them is overweight, they might say they are "fat"; if they see someone with a physical disability, they may be quick to point out the obvious and question it loudly. They are devoid of "political correctness" or insight. This means teaching how to address the subject of honesty tempered with tact.

For instance

- When questioning about a characteristic of someone else, this should be done using an "inside voice" and questions should be directed to the parent or other authority figure quietly versus the person in question.
- Before making a statement about someone else, first put your finger on your lips (a physical reminder) and ask yourself, "How would I feel if this was said about me?" This serves as a consistent reminder of the old adage "If you don't have something nice to say, don't say anything."
- Model tact yourself: if you are someone who uses direct communication to the point of coming across as aggressive, then you must begin to show your child how to tactfully deal with interactions with others in an assertive versus aggressive fashion. Remember, children learn infinitely more by what we do than what we say.

THE EGOCENTRIC NATURE OF CHILDREN

Children tend to be egocentric; that is, they see the moon, the stars, and everyone orbiting in their lives as revolving around their tiny egos. When they are young, they have difficulty understanding the concept of empathy and the possibility of other points of view. It takes burgeoning maturity and reminding via adults demonstrating this complex life skill for them to understand that there are other viewpoints and ways of thinking aside from their own.

This is why the skill of empathy is a crucial and necessary ability to be taught. As a child, the idea of being able to see outside of oneself is counterintuitive. After all, if you are the apple of your parent's eye, shouldn't everyone feel similarly about you? Yet it is those children capable of the ability to grow in empathy and compassionate development early that reap the incredible benefits versus those who are delayed in fostering these skills.

EMPATHY IS BECOMING EXTINCT

Study after study suggests that empathy is in ever shorter supply. Children are becoming more egocentric and less empathetic in their relationships to peers and adults.

For instance

- A study published in 2011 in the *Journal of Personality and Social Psychology Review* found a "decline of 48 percent in college students' scores on empathic concern, a measure of feelings of sympathy, tenderness and compassion for others.[1] There was also a parallel 34 percent decline in perspective-taking (to) imagine another's point of view."[2]
- Konrath and her colleagues took advantage of this wealth of data by collating self-reported empathy scores of nearly fourteen thousand students. She then used a technique known as cross-temporal meta-analysis to measure whether scores have varied over the years. The results were startling: almost 75 percent of students today rate themselves as less empathic than the average student thirty years ago.[3]

SO, WHAT DO WE DO?

The statistics show a definite and important correlation between empathy and success. Conversely, some studies seem to show empathy on the decline. So the question then becomes, how do we inoculate our children from this onslaught of decreasing empathy and improve their futures in developing lasting and meaningful social skills and relationships?

THE "SELFIE" SOCIETY

A relatively recent phenomenon has become the "selfie." The "selfie" has become the virtual self-portrait of the new generation. Look around and you will see teenagers smiling, posing, and twisting in all types of positions to model in their own photo shoot. It may be a tropical destination, with a celebrity, or just to say, "Hey, I am here." It seems innocuous, but in reality, it is the opposite of empathetic behavior; after all, it's called a "selfie," not an "unselfie."

When you are taking a "selfie," you are unlikely to notice others or their emotions. As one stares into the camera of their smartphone, they tend to tune out those around them. Also, children who see the selfies of others tend to think that their lives or daily activities are not as glamorous as those of their peers who manufacture their image in the lens of a smartphone and in the forum of social media.

The warm glow of the smartphone is akin to a flame to a moth for our next generation. Simply looking up and looking out toward peers goes a long way to putting their finger on the pulse of those around them.

TEACH CHILDREN HOW GOOD THEY HAVE IT

The mission statement for parenting at its bare bones, in reality, is quite simple. Provide a child with a roof over their head, food on the table, clothing on their backs, and love to fill their heart. Yet children have taken this a step further to mean a smartphone in their hand, a flat-screen television in their room, and the best brand-name clothes on their backs.

As a result of this competitive nature to have more and more, as adults we have competitively responded to this by giving more and more. It has become an expectation to have the materialistic items for both child and parent alike. One does not want to be left out in the cold with a non-brand-name item and risk the scorn of their peers.

It will not occur to a child to be empathetic if they only are able to see the small world of seeking the latest item(s), especially if they do not realize that others do not have these things. As adults we seek to support the learning of our children in public education. Sometimes, however, in all the extracurricular activities and school events, we forget that just as important an element is to support the expansion of their vision to understanding how others live and compassion for those who struggle in our communities. This means teaching our children service to others. This can be accomplished by the following:

- Take your children to places in which they can provide community service to others that are less fortunate than they are such as a food bank.
- Encourage their participation in activities that provide organized philanthropic activities such as Boy Scouts or Girl Scouts.
- Have them sacrifice something that is important to them to another child or organization to develop the idea of sharing with others who are less fortunate.

- Model for your children using empathy through watching you serve others and making it a point to discuss this with them accordingly.
- Use social media and television as an opportunity to open a dialogue to their opinion and thoughts on stories of others that have less than they do and encourage them to be in touch with their emotions in regard to this.
- When a child has an idea to give or help others (provided it is safe and within your discretion), support them.
- Teach children service to their family through chores. Chores are a means of learning how to help others and demonstrate that they are a valued, necessary, and important member of the family "team."

YOU ARE NEVER TOO YOUNG TO VOLUNTEER

It is typical for children to live in a "me" society—"what is in it for me?" This is compounded by the fact that children are initially noted to have thinking (as we have discussed) associated with the belief that everything that goes on in their world is somehow personalized to something they did or did not do. Parenting styles, likewise, have also transformed; we tend to hover over our children. This can lend itself to stifling the ability for a child to look outside one's self.

There is a very real danger associated with children who continue to seek or believe that the world revolves around them. As they enter the environment of school, in which peers also seek the teacher's limited attention, they become angered and jealous. Sometimes these same children seek to "cut to the chase" and utilize negative attentional behaviors as the easiest means for getting "the biggest bang for the buck."

Volunteering gives children a sense of control and purpose. Think about it. Adults control each and every aspect of their existence: when/what they eat, what they wear, when they wake up, and even when they go to the bathroom. Children are perpetually "one down" in that they are always cared for. The old saying "Children should be seen and not heard" is common enough. It points to a very crucial aspect of a child's life; however, it leaves them thinking, "What is my purpose if everyone is always taking care of me?"

Volunteering turns the tables on that a bit. Now a child has an opportunity to "level the playing field" a bit as they have a voice (albeit small) in the world that they will one day inherit.

The following are some ideas for a child that will allow them the chance to have some role in the world and, in turn, opportunities for confidence building. Keep in mind that safety is paramount in any activity and so, as a parent or educator, exercising good judgment and doing volunteering alongside a child is always the best strategy.

- Consider visiting a nursing home: Elderly persons often crave the vitality and energy of youth. Many of the nursing homes have an activity director that can provide a list of scheduled activities that you and your child can join in on or assist with. Doing so teaches your child that the elderly are persons of wisdom, deserving of respect, and that they can learn a lot from a previous generation. Additionally, it teaches children about the cycle of life and allows you to discuss firsthand some life lessons (if age appropriate in nature).
- Help at a local food pantry: Our children often take the most basic items for granted: food, shelter, clothing. Yet the most basic of items are the most vital for us all. An eye-opening experience is to take them to donate food directly to a food pantry and explain the purpose for these important social service resources.
- Go to the library: The library is a wonderful place to blend a love of reading with activities. Offering to help in a library is a win-win situation for all as you are instilling community with the joy of books.
- Locate local scouting opportunities: Scouting provides an organized opportunity for your child to develop a sense of philanthropy and leadership among their peers. These organizations often incorporate volunteering into their activities.
- Utilize religious activities: Religious-based charitable activities often tie nicely into meeting the spiritual, charitable, and empathy needs of a child and can be done in the context of a family.
- Encourage thank-you notes, pictures, and cards: Having your child draw pictures, notes, or cards to people in the hospital, troops far away, or those that are not able to get out of their home is a wonderful way to put their artistic and empathetic talents to good use.
- Have your children see you volunteer: If you do not volunteer, your child will not see the purpose of doing so within the paradigm of their own life. Explain to them the importance of "giving back."

TO BE EMPATHETIC AND COMPASSIONATE, YOU MUST FIRST UNDERSTAND FEELINGS

Each child varies in their emotional aptitude. Emotional intelligence (EQ or EI) is a term created by two researchers—Peter Salovey and John Mayer—and popularized by Dan Goleman in his 1996 book of the same name.[4] EQ or EI is defined as the ability to: (a) recognize, understand, and manage our own emotions, and (b) recognize, understand, and influence the results of your actions upon the emotions of others.

In a 2013 article in *Forbes* magazine, the writers found that a research study by Carnegie Institute of Technology concluded 85 percent of financial achievement is due to skills like your personality, ability to communicate, and demonstrated leadership (EQ skills). This is versus the common IQ skills, only 15 percent of which they deemed "technical knowledge."[5]

BUILDING THE EMOTIONAL INTELLIGENCE OF A CHILD

Making your child more aware of their emotions and the complexity of these feelings can help build EQ/EI. Additionally, sharing with your child your own emotions and why you feel the way you do can help in also enhancing their own ability to read the emotional atmosphere that surrounds them. Finally, even something as simple as watching television and questioning the "mood/emotion" of each character can draw EQ/EI even in recreational moments.

This will also help your child when feelings seem to "come out of the blue." For instance, the youth becomes sad and angry. Yet they cannot seem to identify what it is that is bothering them. By a discussion and practice of studying the feelings of themselves and others, they can more readily identify what is going on for them. They will also begin to recognize combinations of feelings such as mad + sad = frustration, excited + nervous = anxious, and so on.

HELP THE CHILD TO REALIZE WHEN THEY ARE GOING DOWN THE WRONG EMOTIONAL PATH

Be honest; when they have said something inappropriate to the situation or made a joke that is not in the correct context, it is vital that they receive immediate feedback. If your child does not get that rapid feedback, they are likely to carry on down the road of inappropriate or insensitive comments. Swift response means rapid return back to a more appropriate social pathway.

ASK QUESTIONS

While we will discuss the formation of asking questions for communication skills later in this book, the idea of simply being open to asking questions of others is a key to developing empathy. Often, especially younger children mistake questions for statements. So when told to ask a question (or if they have a question), they will simply make a statement or tell a story.

Formulation of open-ended questions is a key to getting youth to be able to understand another peer's world.

EDUCATIONAL APPLICATION

Some of our students live in worlds that we cannot imagine. Right outside the doors of every school (yes, including yours) are issues in which families are struggling to put food on the table, have no water or power, or experience domestic violence as well as abuse and neglect. When we go home at night, these are the children that make us toss and turn wondering what they are going through and if they are going to be sitting at their desk tomorrow.

Our children live in isolated worlds. Some of them are exposed to more than we can imagine, while others are not exposed to anything at all due to being overly protected. Yet we want them to have some degree of realizing what their fellow children may be going through so that they can develop the so vital humanistic trait of empathy.

While developing the trait of empathy into your curricular programming in your school, keep in mind the following:

- Seek reading and stories of those that have overcome adversity: Helping a child to understand adversity and troubles that others have triumphed over allows them to feel for that person (real or fictional).
- Encourage philanthropic organizations involvement: In our communities, there are a great number of civic organizations doing amazing things for those less fortunate. Teaming with them and having them share these stories when appropriate gives our pupils a more open perspective of the world that is outside their own.

- Model empathy: Many times the problems and issues that students are experiencing seem less vital or catastrophic then those of adults. Therefore, as adults we minimize or downplay them. Encouraging students to share their stories and modeling understanding and empathy carry things a long way.
- Celebrate empathy: When you see students who gather around a crying peer and offer to help and support them, this is worthy of praise and celebration. Consider praising these "events" individually, in a small group, or with assemblies. Empathy is a trait that is so often pushed to the back burner in the heat of a competitive world.

NOTES

1. Sarah H. Konrath, Edward H. O'Brien, and Courtney Hsing, "Changes in Dispositional Empathy in American College Students over Time: A Meta-Analysis," *Personality and Social Psychology Review* 15, no. 2 (2010): 180–98, http://journals.sagepub.com/doi/abs/10.1177/1088868310377395.

2. Dennis Krebs, "Empathy and Altruism," *Journal of Personality and Social Psychology* 32, no. 6 (1975): 1134–46, doi:10.1037//0022-3514.32.6.1134.

3. Konrath et al., "Changes in Dispositional Empathy in American College Students over Time."

4. Peter Salovey, Marc A. Brackett, and John D. Mayer, eds., *Emotional Intelligence: Key Readings on the Mayer and Salovey Model* (Port Chester, NY: National Professional Resources, 2004).

5. Keld Jensen, "Intelligence Is Overrated: What You Really Need to Succeed," Forbes, November 13, 2012, https://www.forbes.com/sites/keldjensen/2012/04/12/intelligence-is-overrated-what-you-really-need-to-succeed.

Chapter Five

We're All the Same

Teaching Our Children to Dive into the Melting Pot of Tolerance

> Love is not just tolerance. It's not just distant appreciation. It's a warm sense of, "I am enjoying the fact that you are you." —N. T. Wright

CHILD PROFILE

Janet is a thirteen-year-old middle school student. She has been in trouble numerous times for harassing, intimidating, and bullying other children in her class. She has made fun of the students who are learning to speak English by mocking their accents. Additionally, she has been noted to tease other children regarding their physical appearance and especially targets those with disabilities (despite that she also has a mild learning disability).

Her parents are at wit's end as they realize that this behavior has led her to a string of detentions and now suspensions. Her actions have become a source of confusion and embarrassment for them. They try to talk to her; however, she replies over and over again, "I don't care. I don't like them!" As a direct result, this behavior has increasingly isolated her from all those around her.

Chapter 5

THE IMPORTANCE OF TOLERATING TOLERANCE

As the Internet grows, the distance between any areas of the world concurrently decreases. If in the past parents may have thought that understanding, culture, and tolerance were just a nice way for us to make our children seem more "polished and cultured," that is no longer the case. Now, cultural diversity, tolerance, and understanding are key elements for success if children are going to learn to swim in the melting pot of life and the world. Additionally, that melting pot is one that will enrich all that allow themselves a dip in its streams.

IF YOU DON'T TEACH CHILDREN DIVERSITY AND TO COEXIST, THE FUTURE WILL NOT BE AS BRIGHT FOR THEM

According to the *Huffington Post*, racial and cultural dynamics are changing rapidly: "Just half a century ago, less than three percent of new marriages were between people of different races; today, 15.5 percent of newlyweds come from different racial backgrounds."[1]

Further, according to the website *Slate*, "Come 2050, only 47 percent of Americans will call themselves white, while the majority will belong to a minority group. Blacks will remain steady at 13 percent of the population, while Asians will grow to 8 percent. Hispanics, on the other hand, will explode to 28 percent of all U.S. population, up from 19 percent in 2010."[2]

This means not only will diversity and tolerance enrich our country, but our youth will need to be aware of how to navigate and understand a multitude of perspectives, cultures, and traditions. Being "worldly" or "cultured" will soon not be just a nice trait to supplement a child's repertoire of talents. Soon, the need to understand and empathize with a global paradigm of thought will be an absolute necessity.

TOLERANCE STARTS AT HOME

Children have an innate curiosity toward new things. Additionally, they don't see the prejudices that are placed upon relationships—we as adult do that. This means that we must be cautious regarding our individual stereotypes or prejudices, which become viral contagions that spread to our children like wildfire.

Instead, it is best to embrace and try to understand cultures along with your child. When they ask a question as to why people do this or that, don't discount the request; help your child to figure out traditions. Find out why people do what they do. Researching a culture or a tradition is now for the first time at the simple fingertips of us all.

GO TO CULTURAL EVENTS

Giving your child the opportunity to attend cultural events expands their horizons. If your child only wanted pizza, chicken nuggets, and mac and cheese, would you accept that? Probably not, because you know that it takes a balanced and multifaceted diet for them to grow and thrive.

Likewise, if your child were only to experience one culture that they are familiar with, could they fully grow and thrive? It would seem just as necessary that they understand the full diet of nourishment in the domain of global identities, traditions, and practices.

UNDERSTANDING HOLIDAYS THAT ARE DIFFERENT THAN YOUR OWN

The New Jersey Department of Education recognizes "more than one hundred holidays of varying cultures throughout the academic year."[3] Now, it is not possible to know all the holidays (major and minor) that are celebrated throughout a year. However, one should know the chief holidays for each major culture. This is especially true if you work in a school district that has a particularly high population of one culture or another.

Even if you are of the same general religion, there are several different types and sects of that same religion that celebrate holidays in very different manners. The following list contains just a small sampling of the many types of religions and holidays that are recognized among various persons throughout the world and in the United States. Encouraging a child to look at the various manners of observing these holidays and events gives a better idea of the systemic nature around the globe of tolerance and understanding.

January
Gatan-sai (New Year's) (religion/culture: Shinto)
Makar Sankranti (religion/culture: Hindu)
Mawlid-al-Nabi (Muhammad's birthday) (religion/culture: Islam)

Russian Orthodox Christmas (religion/culture: Eastern Christian)
Solemnity of Mary, the Mother of God (religion/culture: Catholic)

February
Holi (religion/culture: Hindu)
Imbolc (religion/culture: Wiccan)
Lantern Festival (religion/culture: Chinese cultural festival)
Lunar New Year (religion/culture: China and other Asian countries)
Maha Sivaratri (Shiva's Night) (religion/culture: Hindu)
Nowruz (religion/culture: Middle Eastern/Central Asian)
Purim (religion/culture: Judaism)
Vernal Equinox/Ostara (religion/culture: Wiccan/Pagan)

April
Eastern Orthodox Christian Easter (religion/culture: Eastern Orthodox Christian)
First Day of the Ridvan Festival (religion/culture: Baha'i)
Hanuman Jayanti (religion/culture: Hindu)
Ninth Day of the Ridvan Festival (religion/culture: Baha'i)
Passover (religion/culture: Judaism)
Qing Ming (Tomb Sweeping Day) (religion/culture: Chinese Cultural Festival)

May
Beltane (religion/culture: Pagan/Wiccan)
Eid al-Fitr (religion/culture: Islam)
Ramadan (religion/culture: Islam)
Shavuot (religion/culture: Judaism)
Twelfth Day of the Ridvan Festival (religion/culture: Baha'i)

CONSIDER MENTORING A FOREIGN STUDENT

For some, taking the plunge of having a student from another country is a great way for your child to see and understand the world by bringing it into your home. A word of caution: make certain that this is a good fit for your family. Having anyone living within your home is a deeply personal decision.

ENCOURAGE LEARNING ANOTHER LANGUAGE

Many children do not see the purpose of learning a secondary language. Yet most youth from other countries are fluent in several other languages and dialects (including English). In fact according to a *Forbes* article written by David Skorton and Glenn Altschuler, quoting Arnie Duncan, former U.S. Department of Education secretary, "Only 18% of Americans report speaking a language other than English, while 53% of Europeans can converse in a second language."[2] Hence, learning a foreign language is not only a means to better developing cultural awareness but also a way to get "a leg up" in a world that is ever changing and globally competitive.

EXPLORE CULTURAL FESTIVALS, MUSIC, AND RESTAURANTS

The easiest means of sharing a culture is through food and/or music. Visiting different restaurants and cultural events allows your child to experience cultures and celebration in a new and exciting way. Many towns have cultural festivals to highlight the varying cultures that populate their regions.

TRAVEL TO PLACES

When you travel to places regionally or, if you have the opportunity, internationally, point out differences, similarities, and the reasons the people in the respective regions do what they do. Ask questions, be respectful, and learn alongside your child.

TALK ABOUT TOLERANCE AND PREJUDICE

Often, the topic of tolerance and prejudice is a subject many don't address with their children (if they are not a minority) unless it becomes something they are forced to discuss and acknowledge. Discrimination, however, is an unfortunate reality of life that cannot be ignored.

Holidays such as Martin Luther King Jr. Day or Holocaust Memorial Day (every January 27) are suitable times to address the topic in an age-appropriate fashion.

REMEMBER BLAME, JUDGMENT, AND INTIMIDATION COME FROM FEAR, FRUSTRATION, AND DIMINISHED SELF-ESTEEM

Do not allow your child to use fear, anger, or resentment to generate an attitude of blame or a belief of generating and directing negative emotions toward others (versus addressing how they could take personal responsibility).

Encouraging self-responsibility avoids an "us versus them mentality." When any of us judge and blame, it tends to create an atmosphere of intolerance as "someone has got to be blamed and it can't be me."

AVOID JOKES THAT ARE OVERLY RACY OR MAY BE RACIST

Many jokes that are told in the adult world may have an undertone that pokes fun at various different types of persons and beliefs. Different people find various forms of comedic relief humorous. The difficulty is most of this humor rests on subtlety and tact as to its application. Additionally, it relies on sarcasm to get the point across.

These are skills that children do not tend to possess nor understand. Therefore, it is best to reinforce for children that if not everyone finds it funny, it is simply not funny. Come to think of it, this may be good advice for the adult world as well.

QUESTIONS SHOULD BE ANSWERED

Children are creatures of constant questions. "Why?" can be the constant mantra of a child (particularly a younger one). These inquiries often occur when they come to their mind with no regard for the social graces or timing of the adult world.

When these inquiries are made, frequently they are at times when adults feel they are inappropriate or not at the most comfortable of times. This embarrassment often leads adults to sweep the well-meaning requests under the rug. This, in turn, makes a child feel they should not inquire about differences between themselves and others because it may be wrong or shameful.

EDUCATIONAL APPLICATION

Children do not learn prejudice in a vacuum; they learn it from the environment that places stereotypes and negative connotations to others who think, look, or speak differently than ourselves. Ultimately, it is adults that place the barometer on a child's level of acceptance of others.

For many children, however, their first experience into interacting with others who are decidedly different than themselves occurs in the halls and classrooms of public school. This makes tolerance not a side element of school success but a central one. Using some of the below ideas may be useful in the integration of this into the daily school day.

- Encourage children's differences: As a child, many of our youth simply want to "fit in." Encourage difference in thought, language, and culture.
- Seek diverse curriculum: Don't stick to the curriculum that only addresses familiar cultures and practices. Should your district policy allow, seek stories from different places with characters that are not familiar or traditional.
- Discuss transformational characters in history who broke racial or ethnic barriers and were hallmarks for tolerance: Children are very often aware of "superheroes"; however, they are not as versed in heroes like Martin Luther King, Gandhi, Rosa Parks, and a host of others who made a difference through tolerance.
- Allow students to share differences: If a student would like to share about their culture or why they do what they do, allow this and, if they feel comfortable, provide time if others have appropriate questions.
- Encourage kindness and the "golden rule" as universal: Though we want to address differences and understanding, the theme of kindness should be one that is woven through all lessons and a common humanity.

NOTES

1. Sofia Espinoza Alvarez, "Conversing over the Dynamics of American Multiculturalism," *Huffington Post*, June 12, 2017, https://www.huffingtonpost.com/entry/conversing-over-the-dynamics-of-american-multiculturalism_us_58ea4deee4b00dd8e016ecfb.

2. Jamelle Bouie, "Will Today's Hispanics Be Tomorrow's Whites?" *Slate Magazine*, April 15, 2014, http://www.slate.com/articles/news_and_politics/politics/2014/04/america_s_future_racial_makeup_will_today_s_hispanics_be_tomorrow_s_whites.html.

3. List of Religious Holidays Permitting Pupil Absence from School, http://www.state.nj.us/education/genfo/holidays.htm.

4. David Skorton and Glenn Altschuler, "America's Foreign Language Deficit," *Forbes*, August 27, 2012, https://www.forbes.com/sites/collegeprose/2012/08/27/americas-foreign-language-deficit.

Chapter Six

Making a Good First, Second, and Third Impression

The Importance of Hygiene

My belief is you have one chance to make a first impression —Kevin McCarthy

CHILD PROFILE

Sammy is a ten-year-old boy who believes his sole job in school is to make other kids laugh. He sneezes and wipes it on his sleeve, and when his fellow students gasp and chuckle to themselves, he believes he is funny. He will often pass gas in the middle of his class and finds it funny when everyone turns and looks at him.

Sammy often forgets to brush or wash his hair, leaving the long, greasy curls to flop across his head. He wears pants that are too big and fall, resulting in his underwear hanging out. Sammy often smells like body odor, and despite his peers literally running away from him, he does not understand why they do not want to spend time with him.

Sammy can be found at recess by himself, cautiously at the perimeter, uncertain as to how to get attention in a positive way. Sometimes other children will dare him to do something humiliating, which he will gladly do for just a small glimmer of attention.

A FIRST IMPRESSION IS A VITAL IMPRESSION

The impression that a child makes on his peers, teachers, and coworkers is extremely important. Dr. Sean Horan, in an article for *Psychology Today*, reports, "We may need just a few seconds to form an accurate and reliable judgment about another person."[1]

What happens if those "few seconds" are a youth trying to make a friend, developing an impression on a teacher, or in the moments interviewing for a first job? A large part of that is visual, and therefore, hygiene is a critical framework that can (and should be) looked at.

TEACH IT EARLY AND OFTEN

Children initially are more open to the lessons of hygiene. Generally, these lessons are naturally employed into the routine of preschool, and they openly accept learning about cleanliness. Therefore, take advantage of this and utilize this both at school and at home by educating them and being consistent in this important area.

GENDER-SPECIFIC DISCUSSIONS

To avoid discomfort, common sense would indicate that it is best that same-gender parents or educators discuss these sensitive issues with children as necessary.

PEOPLE MAKE ASSUMPTIONS ABOUT LACK OF HYGIENE

According to Melissa Conrad Stöppler, in a web article in Medicine.Net, "People may develop poor hygiene habits due to social factors such as poverty or inadequacy of social support,"[2] thereby visually creating a virtual self-fulfilling prophecy of social withdrawal for those that are seeking friendship and socialization.

THE WORLD THAT YOU CAN'T SEE

Out of sight, out of mind. Only a century ago, what you did not see could, and did, kill you. Countless people died from the smallest of enemies: germs. Doctors then tried everything from bloodletting to medical remedies and many methods that we would find barbaric today. Yet they could not see the germs that were insidiously eating away at the lives of those around them.

What does this have to do with hygiene? Educating children about germs and the importance of cleanliness can provide, from an educational vantage point, an idea of why hygiene is important for their overall health.

TEACHING HOW TO WASH HANDS

It may seem simple to wash your hands. However, a child with deficient social skills also may not be aware of the importance of these skills. They throw some water on their hands (if lucky) and dry them on their jeans and they are off again.

What if they are seeking a food service job or doing volunteer activities that involve food? This now puts their livelihood or volunteer jaunt at risk. Therefore, sometimes the little things do become the big things. Or what if their peers see them not wash their hands and accuse them of being unclean or slovenly?

Encourage your child to use soap and water and sing the "Happy Birthday" song. Why? This song's length is the approximate length of time necessary to appropriately wash one's hands.

CONSIDER USING PROFESSIONALS FOR HYGIENE LESSONS

Many times youth will listen to those who are not their immediate parent. If you ever had the experience in which you have told your child over and over some nugget of wisdom that you have tried to get across to them, only to find that a teacher or coach tells them once and they treat it like some sage-like wisdom, you understand this.

Having the pediatrician, the dentist, or the teacher talk to them about proper hygiene may sometimes be the different paradigm necessary to help get the message across.

HAVE YOUR CHILD TAKE RESPONSIBILITY FOR HYGIENE

Often a child has a hygiene routine in the morning. Coincidentally, this is also the most stressful time for a household as everyone is shuffling to get out the door in the morning. This becomes troublesome as the time that a child may need your attention most you are available least (getting yourself or other siblings ready).

Therefore, a youth must remember the procedure or have some manner to recall what they should do. Consider using a digital camera and having them take pictures of their hygiene routine (thereby teaching responsibility). Items such as brushing your teeth, showering, and using deodorant can be represented by photos of the toothbrush, the showerhead, and finally the deodorant.

Now printing these pictures and placing them in an obvious place provides a constant reminder of what to do in terms of hygiene and order of such. Sometimes, due to thoughts of what will be going on for the day, exhaustion, or other distraction, it takes this kind of concrete reminder(s).

BREAK DOWN

Sometimes it is an issue of quality. Those with developmental issues want to have appropriate hygiene; however, they lack the ability initially to do so with the quality necessary. Therefore, breaking it down to measurable bites that they can absorb may be a necessary component for them to master these skills.

ALLOW THE CHILD TO SAVE FACE

When a youth is caught doing something embarrassing, like scratching their backside or putting their finger up their nose, making them aware in public only adds to the potential shame and embarrassment. Rather than calling them out on it, allow them to save face.

Whispering quietly to the offending youth or providing some physical sign will help from making an uncomfortable moment all the more so. Likewise discussion of hygiene should be done out of the earshot of the eager ears of peers.

INCLUDE HYGIENE ITEMS AT SCHOOL

To avoid issues of potential embarrassment and educational purposes, it may be prudent to have items handy for them to utilize in school when appropriate.

WHY DO I NEED TO DO THIS?

The need to maintain good hygiene may seem obvious. However, if my main goal is to play with my friends, watch television, or do some other activity, hygiene seems a meaningless waste of my time. Therefore we have to make sure that we detail this for these children.

Important reasons to maintain good self-care include the following

- you want to get and maintain a job (if of applicable age),
- you want to avoid peers teasing or staying away from you,
- you want to smell good so potential friends want to go near you.

HYGIENE SHOULD BE AN IMPORTANT PART OF CURRICULUM

In most schools, health is integrated into the existing curriculum. Delving into appropriate hygiene lessons is key. This is especially topical as prepubescent teens may not realize the impending need for deodorant and other hygiene needs as they change.

BUY POTENTIAL ITEMS OF EMBARRASSMENT

Some items may simply be too embarrassing or a youth may not think to ask for (nor wish to spend their "own money" on) such items. Purchasing these items when the time has come will cut down on the anxiety of a growing adolescent needing to do so initially.

These include items such as

- deodorant,
- feminine products,
- shaving items.

SOMETIMES THE HARDEST WAY IS THE BEST WAY

At times, the natural consequence is far more effective (though hard to witness) than anything you can say to a child. For instance, how many times did your parent say, "When I was your age (fill in the blank)"?

Was this ever effective? More than likely, you simply discarded this wise, sagely advice as useless banter. So it is with suggestions given to the next generation of youth. The singular consequence of being told "you smell" or "you're a slob" from a peer will provide a far more effective consequence then anything an adult can say.

SCHOOL APPLICATION

In school the pupil who stands out due to being unclean or having less than stellar hygiene can quickly become a subject of bullying or, at the very least, isolation from the judging glare of certain peers. Good hygiene is a skill that will not only assist a student in avoiding this but also allow a child to avoid being lumped into a stereotype of being uncaring or unmotivated. To assist with hygiene, consider the following:

- Can the family afford what is needed? For some students, the few pairs of tattered clothes may be all they have in their drawers at home. Having the school counselor offer assistance for resources may be a necessary and important means of allowing a student to have appropriate fitting and fresh clothing.
- Does the student know? We often assume, "Doesn't that kid know his shirt is inside out and his collar is half up and half down?" The answer may, in fact, be no! How many times have you walked unaware that you have a big green piece of spinach in your teeth? If you see an issue, talk to the child in private, and this may help them to be aware of their hygiene.
- Use the nurse: Continued poor hygiene becomes a medical issue. The nurse can have a discussion with the student and parent about the health applications of a lack of cleanliness.
- Incorporate it into the health curriculum: In most schools, the physical education/health teacher discusses this with students in their lessons. If not, consider it a necessary group lesson.

NOTES

1. Sean M. Horan, "Do You Need Your Partner to Be a Mind Reader?" *Psychology Today*, January 14, 2015, http://www.psychologytoday.com/blog/adventures-in-dating/201501/do-you-need-your-partner-be-mind-reader.

2. Melissa Conrad Stöppler, "Poor Hygiene: Symptoms & Signs," https://www.medicinenet.com/poor_hygiene/symptoms.htm.

Chapter Seven

Fishing for Friends

A Hard Catch

> Friendships in childhood are usually a matter of chance, whereas in adolescence they are most often a matter of choice. —David Elkind

CHILD PROFILE

Madelyn is a ten-year-old who spends most of her time at home watching television. She wants to have friends like everyone else, but she has a paralyzing fear of calling other peers.

Madelyn has a few acquaintances at school that she spends time with, however, she does not know how to make the leap from that environment to friendships and play dates. She stays at home most weekends or does chores around the house.

Her solitude has made her very sad. She wants to reach out to others but simply does know not how to do it. She is quiet and afraid to ask for help, so she will often simply retreat to her bedroom and cry in lonely silence into her pillow in a lonely world of her own four walls.

IMPORTANCE OF FRIENDSHIP IN CHILDHOOD

In childhood, we develop foundations for lifelong friendship as well as socialization skills. Children learn to develop memories, find out how to play, and establish conflict resolution skills that take them well down the road of development into adulthood.

For some youngsters, childhood is a journey that is relatively smooth and friends are developed with ease. For others, this takes time and is a cautious trek of uncertainty and confusion.

INTROVERSION OR EXTROVERSION?

There is a very real belief by society that those adults (and children) who are extroverted and overtly social are better adjusted to life than those who tend to be more reserved and introverted. Superficially, some may see this as the case; however, it is important to recognize that these are simply two very different perspectives for looking at the world around you.

Introverted children

- Tend to prefer one-to-one conversations and play interactions.
- Seek deeper connections with relatively fewer peers.
- Are generally more accurate in understanding peer relationships.
- May prefer family relationships over spending time with peers.
- Like to choose adult conversation versus child-to-child discussions.
- Would rather have short, limited periods of socializing as it is taxing to them for extended time frames.
- Tend to like to do more reading, listening, and reflecting.
- Like predictability and routine.
- Do not, generally, want unnecessary attention.
- May be a first or only child.

Extroverted children

- Enjoy multiple relationships with peers at once.
- Tend to like more superficial "small talk."
- Do not express as much interest in understanding the relational dynamics as the context of communication.
- May prefer peers/friends to family.
- Sometimes want to have child-to-child versus adult conversation.
- Gain energy and enjoyment from prolonged socializing.
- May be more animated and be lighthearted.

- Prefer "flying by the seat of their pants" versus rigidly preplanned activities.
- Like more attention and enjoy "being the life of the party."
- Not often an only or first child.

Of course, children (as well as adults) operate along a spectrum of being more or less outgoing. It is rare that any child is totally introverted or extroverted, nor is either trait characteristically inherently "good or bad."

WHERE DO CHILDREN GROW FRIENDS?

- Look for common interests: Often children can bond over shared hobbies. Schools; churches, synagogues, mosques, and temples; and libraries often provide clubs based on common interests.
- Look for organized activities that allow for socialization: Children are often provided opportunities in our current generation for sports, crafts, and a host of other activities. The adults in their respective lives should seek activities that not only give instruction in the selected activity but also provide less structured times for youth to stretch their "social wings."
- Look for activities that offer positive character traits integrated into their curriculum: Groups such as Boy Scouts, Girl Scouts, religious groups, and child-based civic organizations often infuse important character education elements into their lessons and activities that are positive attributes toward a child's ultimate social and character growth.
- Plan play dates with age-appropriate peers: If you have friends or relatives that have children that are in the same approximate age group, giving them an opportunity to socialize can be useful. Keep in mind that trying social skills may mean that sometimes conflict or disagreement arises. Being in earshot can help you coach and develop better means of social problem solving.

CONSIDER PARENT SUPPORT GROUPS

Nothing can be more frustrating or heartbreaking than to watch a child voyage out into the world, only to be sunk by the icebergs of rejection from those around them. More and more, however, a growing number of children are finding difficulty with social skills and less and less is it easy to provide strong character traits necessary to develop strong adults for our next generation.

Hence, parenting support groups can be a good means of finding children that have the same needs as your child as well as a way of finding interventions idiosyncratic to your child's community. Such groups also provide a means of enriching mothers and fathers who empathize with the frustration their child is experiencing.

MENTORS DO NOT NEED TO ALWAYS BE ADULTS

Keep in mind that mentoring does not always have to come from adults. In fact, it probably is more effective from another youth who "speaks the language of children" and is immersed in their world. Therefore, having mentors in the school and/or other settings will provide a good means of role modeling socialization challenges they face to uncertain youth. Not to mention, a younger mentor experiences the youth's culture in "real time" versus when adult mentors witness the same culture, which is skewed by kids who "tend to be on their best behavior." This also allows children to be introduced to peers by peers and opens additional more natural opportunities for relational interactions of a positive nature.

TECHNOLOGY FRIENDS DO NOT MAKE GOOD SLEEPOVER PARTNERS

Some children seek to find "virtual friends" versus flesh and blood relationships. That is, they find friends via video games, social media, and texting. The difficulty is that these relationship qualities are very limited. They are emotionally more safe in that the contact is limited as well as superficial and do not require the challenges or complexity of a true face-to-face friendship. Yet, they are also thoroughly unsatisfying as they do not allow for nonverbal communications and are limited in what these relationships can foster (i.e., you cannot have a solely social media friend over for dinner or a sleepover).

FOCUSING ON THE WHO, WHAT, WHEN, WHY, AND HOW

A key to development of friendships is asking questions. Yet children that demonstrate low or stunted social skills often are uncertain about this very aptitude.

For instance, when you request that a child ask a question, they will often instead tell a story or make a statement. This is certainly not as conducive to relational development as questions for how you get to know another peer.

Teaching a child, however, to initiate a sentence with "who," "what," "when," "why," or "how" provides a different slant. It offers a more forced emphasis toward developing questions versus making statements.

Practicing starting a sentence with one of these words will help to verbally "force" developing these skills accordingly. Simply ask that the phrase be started by a key inquiry word to create the building of friendship dialogue questions.

DEVELOP AN INTRODUCTION

Some children have no trouble introducing themselves to others. In fact, they are overzealous in trying to speak with anyone in earshot and tell them anything and everything about themselves. This socially "pushy" nature creates a point that embarrasses or turns off the other youth.

It seems obvious that introductions are the opening to a conversation. However, if a child becomes anxious or uncertain, even the items that seem simplistic can be difficult to recall. Therefore, it is important to more rigidly script an introduction for some.

For instance,

- Simply saying hello: That seems all too simplistic. Yet this is often the easiest means of entering a conversation. Often, the simplest responses are forgotten in favor of what seems more complex and unnecessary. Sometimes, however, the anticipatory anxiety of saying anything but "hi" for a child makes this the only viable option.
- Finding an opportunity to make a compliment: Asking a child to make a positive personalized compliment in a greeting can start the conversation in an appropriate direction. Have a child provide accolades of what a peer is skilled at, something they wear/have, or any other attribute to put the other youngster at ease via flattery.
- Ask questions: Remember, teach that sentences that begin with "who," "what," "when," "why," and "how" can lead to inquiring versus leading conversations down a one-way street of the child droning on about themselves.

- Avoid "I" messages and encourage "you" messages: Those that are weak in interactional skills sometimes tend to talk only about themselves through "I" messages (which are best for conflict resolution). If they start with "you," it invites an open-ended conversation.

CONVERSATIONAL SKILLS: THE BUILDING BLOCKS OF RELATIONSHIPS

Eye Contact

Often we equate eye contact with paying attention and good listening skills. Yet, in many aspects, eye contact can also be utilized as a means of intimidating in certain contexts. Conversely, some children find it intimidating to look directly into the eye of another. Teaching the child to look at the other party's nose can accomplish the same goal with far less anxiety.

Proper Distance

Often the appropriate distance in most communication is approximately eighteen to twenty-four inches for optimal comfort between both parties. Have your child get in the habit of extending their arm and hand. If they are touching someone without using their fingertips, they are likely too close. After demonstrating these skills for a period of time, then they can practice using an "imaginary" arm and estimating the distance accordingly.

Reflective Listening

When teaching questions, get in the habit of patterning reflective listening and imparting this skill. When the child that you are trying to teach states something, attempt to clarify it by asking, "So what you are trying to tell me is _____?" After modeling this method of refining and questioning, have the child try it. (See the chapter on conflict resolution skills for more information.)

Interrupting

Youth, and sometimes adults, have issues with interrupting the person speaking. In an effort to not forget what they want to say, the child tries continually to interject their statement into the conversation and attempts to "talk over" the other individual. Try a concrete reminder such as, "When I/you have the pencil (any concrete object), you are allowed to speak. When I am finished, then I will hand you the pencil and then I want to hear what you have to say."

Topics of Conversation

Perhaps the hardest issue is not the conversation skills themselves but what to speak about. It is important that our children have topics on which they can center the framework of a conversation. Topics for conversation starters include

School Based:

- What grade are you in?
- Who is your favorite teacher?
- What is your favorite special (art, gym, music, etc.)?
- What do you like to play at recess?

Personal Based:

- What is your favorite thing to do?
- What school/grade are you in?
- Do you have any brothers/sisters/pets?
- What is your favorite/least favorite thing to learn in school?

Recreation Based:

- Are you involved in any sports? What sports? What is the name of your team(s)?
- What is your favorite book? What are your favorite video games? What is your favorite movie?
- What is your favorite TV show?
- What do you like to do for fun?

Topics That Are "off the Table":

- Any topic that insults someone else.
- Topics related to sex, drugs, politics, or religion.
- Anything that can be deemed gossip or harassing, intimidating, or bullying in nature.

- Starting every sentence with "I" or "me" (i.e., monopolizing an interaction).
- Humor that self-deprecates to the point of affecting the other's self-esteem in a negative fashion.
- Talking negatively about others or self, gossiping, or rumors.

GETTING IN, GETTING OUT, AND EVERYTHING IN THE MIDDLE OF A CONVERSATION

The hardest challenge of conversational skills for children can be the simple task of entering conversation. It is akin to trying to get onto an escalator in that you must step on at the right time or risk stumbling.

So when is the correct time to get onto "the escalator" of conversational skills? Look for a physical opening in the conversation armor: group conversations that show a physical "opening" for which a child can enter the conversation. Conversely, if the group is a closed circle in which the child must "jam" themselves, this is less opportune of an "open" group for talking.

BRIDGING THE GAP BETWEEN SCHOOL AND HOME

Children will often acknowledge that they have friends at school or at the workplace; however, they cannot seem to bridge the gap between transitioning those acquaintances to friendships that are fostered outside the school setting.

Generally, they must be able to use the phone or texting to make this transition from a school acquaintance toward a friendship outside that domain.

To do so, youth must

1. Be able to introduce themselves to whoever answers the telephone.
2. Be able to leave a message should the peer not be available.
3. Schedule plans with the other child and convey time, date, and location (if youth cannot do so, attempt to negotiate a time that they can meet).
4. Recognize that they cannot continue to badger the respective youth if the other child is not willing to meet.
5. Close a conversation politely.

COULD IT BE SOMETHING ELSE?

Many individuals have social anxiety disorders; put simply they are worried to socialize. According to the National Institute of Mental Health, 13.3 percent of adolescents have social phobia/anxiety.[1] It is important then to note that sometimes what seems like social skill deficits may also have integrated into the complexity of issues of anxiety or phobia. If your child is frightened to connect with others (regardless of whether they do have a social skill issue), it is important to consider perhaps getting the advice and guidance of a licensed mental health professional.

BEWARE OF THE WOLF IN FRIEND'S CLOTHING

Children who are extremely eager to find friendships are likely to latch on to whatever youngster will provide them any attention. These children begin to believe any peer attention, positive or negative, is better than no attention at all.

This can lead to issues in which a child bonds to others that may not be quality friends or may be "using" the child for one reason or another. Therefore, if we are going to teach children how to make friends, we must teach them "quality is better than quantity." Additionally, they must be able to begin to "quality assess" potential relationships with a cautious eye.

- More is not necessarily better: Children oftentimes equate more with better. We should help our children to understand a few good friends are better than a multitude of acquaintances.
- Don't compare: Children tend to compare who has more friends and who is more popular. Children should not look at the sheer numbers. Here are the qualities that a child may look to considering before accepting or discarding a growing friendship:

  - Can you trust your friend? Do they do what they say they are going to do? On the other hand, are they one that cancels play dates and/or goes to another friend if the activity looks better?
  - Do they treat you the same in front of other friends? Sometimes kids tend to treat their supposed "friends" differently dependent on the other peers that they are around.

- Are they friends with you when "things are not fun"? A youth may sometimes be friendly when there are fun things going on (e.g., when they are going to an amusement park or the movies). However, if things are not exciting, they abandon their relationships for greener pastures. Conversely, a friend is there when you need them.
- Do they forgive you? All children make mistakes and do things that they regret. It is important, however, that each party in the friendship has an ability to allow the flexibility of mutual forgiveness.

PRUNING RELATIONSHIPS

In the early years of childhood until early adolescence, you can "prune" relationships that your child has. Much like a tree, cutting off certain branches will help the main plant to grow, bloom, and thrive.

If you do not like the looks of certain relationships for your child, simply "cutting back" and/or making those connections less convenient while growing other relationships often works. By "cutting back," this means making rides or time together less able or convenient in favor of other activities or friends. Distance will eventually cause many of these undesired relationships to wither and end.

EDUCATIONAL APPLICATION

Think back to where you made most of your friendships. Most of our childhood friends were made at school. This was the one control place where every one of our same-aged peers gathered together and fostered the commonality and pride of being in the same school community. It is one venue where all had the opportunity to socialize face-to-face for a prolonged length of time.

As educators we seek to foster learning as our primary goal. Simultaneously, many of the children seek socializing, playing, and making friends as their parallel objective. Giving them meaningful opportunities to do this offers them a balance and an ability to be engaged in learning with this base need of connection met as well.

To encourage friendships,

- Point students to seek out those with common interests: Some of our youth with social skills issues have very specific interests. Try to point them

toward peers that have similar hobbies, which will allow them to build a foundation of friendship.
- Remind students when they can socialize: For some youth, they simply cannot wait to talk and socialize. Remind and encourage them toward natural points of socializing during the day.
- Not everyone likes to actively play: Some children at recess would rather read a book or do a quiet activity. Allowing them to do so emboldens those who are more introverted.
- Encourage involvement in extracurricular school activity: Encouraging children to be involved in additional activities outside of school provides a venue in which they can share something in common as well as the potential to make additional friends.

NOTE

1. "Any Anxiety Disorder among Children," National Institute of Mental Health, https://www.nimh.nih.gov/health/statistics/prevalence/any-anxiety-disorder-among-children.shtml.

Chapter Eight

Agreeing to Disagree

Conflict Resolution Skills

The Law of Win/Win says, "Let's not do it your way or my way; let's do it the best way." —Greg Anderson

CHILD PROFILE

Tabitha is a ten-year-old elementary student. She argues with everyone that she meets. She argues that she is right and they are wrong and will not hear of anyone else's point of view. Her friends have deemed her, as a result, a "know-it-all."

Tabitha is difficult in class because she frequently calls out incorrect answers and then disagrees adamantly with the teacher as to why the teacher is wrong and she is absolutely correct. Furthermore, this behavior carries on to her social relationships. She tells her peers what to do and actively "shouts down" any responses that are not in line with her rigid beliefs.

CONFLICT IS A NATURAL PART OF LIFE

Conflict seems almost as natural an element of life as breathing. From when you awake and decide what you (and your children) should wear, to what you are going to have for dinner, to what movie you are going to see this weekend, conflict rears its head again and again.

Of course, there are other conflicts that are less mundane where the stakes are higher. If you are having martial or work issues, your ability to decipher these problems can mean the difference between your success or failure and ultimately your long-term happiness.

ALLOW YOUR CHILD TO EXPERIENCE CONFLICT

Many times the first entry a child has with conflict is through that of their siblings. A child must learn that they cannot always get their way in these situations and then learn conflict resolution.

Sometimes, we attempt to bypass the loud and annoying nature of these arguments by intervening. Other times, we tell the older child, "You should know better; you are older! Give it to him now!" By doing so, we are short-circuiting the ability for both youths to stretch out their wings in the real world of conflict. Also, the question belies, how many times can our kids' conflicts lead us to mirror the behavior of a two-year-old ourselves?

USE OF THE "I" MESSAGE

As we mentioned in the responsibility chapter of the book, the most challenging part of a conflict is taking the heat for what one has done wrong in a disagreement. For many children with poor social skills, this is difficult because they, well intending, attempt to work harder and more aggressively with the more limited tools in their toolbox.

"I" messages are a simple yet effective means of addressing conflict. They have long been used by counselors to help couples deal with the most difficult and sensitive matters, that of marital discord.

The "I" message simply consists of

- Stating "I" (This is vital because you are taking some degree of responsibility in your action/reaction).
- "Feel" (Important because our feelings are objective and aren't inherently right or wrong; they just are).
- "So I would like you to" (Asking for a prospective solution to a problem; avoid placing it in the other's lap to solve and extend an olive branch of a potential answer to the issue at hand).

DO NOT OFFER A COMPLAINT WITHOUT A SOLUTION

In the workplace, supervisors generally look for problem solvers. The new employee does not want to be known as the "problem maker" or the one who creates more work for the boss than they generate for the company.

Ask most who manage people and they will tell you they want those who are motivated to solve a problem with potential solutions versus dropping the problem at the boss's door and expecting them to solve it. Likewise, when a child comes to you with an issue, they are required to have at least one potential solution at hand. It is not simply "tattling" or deferring problem solving to the adult at large. Remember, we are teaching skills that are preparing the child to be a functioning member of the next generation of adults.

TWO EARS, ONE MOUTH

Teaching your children to listen is a vital part of conflict resolution. After all, how do you solve a problem if you don't understand it through using your ears? Therefore, teach your child to listen and reflect back what is being said.

For instance,

Child 1: You cannot play with us! You are always making your own rules to the game, and when we tell you that you are cheating, you yell that we are lying!

Child 2: So, wait, you think I make my own rules in the game?

Child 1: Yes, and we don't like that you call us liars and crybabies!

Child 2: You want me to stop making my own rules and not accuse you of lying?

Child 1: And calling us crybabies!

Child 2: Okay, so I need to stop making my own rules, stop calling you liars and crybabies . . . and then maybe I can play?

Child 1: I guess so . . .

Child 2 is attempting to clarify and understand what is being said and what is needing to be done. They are mirroring ("reflecting") what the peer is asking and continues to refine and clarify it until the problem is crystal clear and, eventually, capable of a solution.

FOCUSING ON WHO IS RIGHT IS WRONG

If you have ever had a heated argument with a significant other, you will know the danger of being "right" in a conflict. Sure, you may have proven yourself like some great defense attorney with your points all lined up neatly in a row, but in the end, you both lose.

Your loved one becomes resentful and upset that you embarrassed them, and although "logically" you are right, "emotionally" you have done more harm than good. Unfortunately, you have learned the lesson the hard way that emotions are not logical and logic has no place in emotions.

WALKING AWAY BEFORE YOU SAY . . .

We have all been there: we are angry and resentful and then we say it. The words that spew forth from our mouths are filled with hate and accusations and maybe sprinkled with some profanities. The recipient is left with the residue of our hateful words and is often surprised by the voracity with which they are fired forth.

Speaking of fired, if those words are aimed at the boss, your days (or minutes) at your job are numbered. Secondly, the careful building of the bridge of relationship that you built with that person over months or years now is engulfed in your fiery rhetoric. In short, the bond is kaput.

So it is with children. They can often allow emotions to get the best of them and then the message or solution they hope to deliver is so heavily seasoned with the heat of anger and scorn that they wind up losing the relationship altogether.

Encouraging a child to wait a few hours and discuss how to address a problem with another may allow some distance from the reactive nature that emotions can cloud in their social skills. Further, discussing and rehearsing with adults they trust on how to specifically frame the manner with which they want to handle a conflict will allow them to decrease the anxiety that they may be harboring.

KEEP IT CLEAN

Children often have trouble distinguishing the argument from the other child. In fact, they may make statements that have nothing to do with the argument and simply are attacks on the other child's looks, character, friends, and so on. These muddy up the conflict and turn it from potentially problem solving to deeply personal and hurtful.

Encourage your child to deal with the issue, not the personality. This can also be role modeled by adults as well since all of us sometimes attack the person versus try to look precisely, and only, at the issue at hand.

A DEAL IS A DEAL

Being "black and white" thinkers, sometimes youth tend to think that they must "win" to have solved an argument. Have the child look at it from a different lens: "Making a deal means you get some (not all) of what you want." Put another way, it is a "win/win" for us both.

DON'T FORGET TO HELP THEM LIGHTEN THE MOOD

Not everything is an emergency, a crisis, or a major conflict. In fact, if everything is a major emergency, then nothing essentially is an emergency. Try to teach children to joke and use self-deprecating humor regarding their actions (not them as a person or this can affect self-esteem) to lighten conflicts. In short, teach them to see the lighter side of life.

TEACH THEM TO FORGIVE

This is a hard one for us as adults, but forgiveness goes a long way. Have you ever had a person who has so irritated you that you think about them morning, noon, and night? Have you ever asked yourself if they are thinking about you all the time as well? Most likely, that's not the case.

Teaching a child to forgive will take the air out of that lingering sense of anger and hatred that will permeate their lives morning, noon, and night. Have them apologize for their part (no matter how small they perceive it to be) and try to reconnect with a relationship that is precious to them. Forgiveness, however, does not have to be correlated with forgetting. If the bond with the other child is one that is constantly marred by a path of hurt and disrespect, then the relationship may need to be terminated at your discretion to preserve your child's self-esteem.

EDUCATIONAL APPLICATION

With so many varied students being tied together in the hustle and bustle of the hallways and classrooms of a public school, there is bound to be disruption and conflict that arises on a regular basis. How this conflict is handled means the difference between successful resolution or physical violence.

If we are going to develop a conflict resolution program in our schools, we must consider the following:

- What are the consequences for not handling conflict appropriately? In the so-called real world, there are consequences and laws to prevent conflict from being handled in a physical manner. The question to ask then is, are the disciplinary measures that a school employs paralleling those of the outside world? If so, how are the consequences an educational deterrent to preventing such a behavior from occurring again?
- Do students know when they cannot handle a conflict? Should a conflict become such that it is in danger of becoming violent, involves someone "being dared," or is considered harassment, intimidation, or bullying, do students know that they are to seek out a faculty member to address that immediately?
- Don't allow a bystander mentality: Often conflict is either fueled or extinguished by the attitude of those around the two arguing. Encourage open discussions about avoidance of gossip and rumors or encouraging fighting and the potential consequences as such.
- Consider a conflict resolution curriculum: Having an outcome-based conflict resolution program as well as monthly character education programs assists students in developing a common language from which to speak about conflict resolution.
- Encourage role-playing: When conflicts do arise, have students role-play potential solutions.
- Be where the conflicts are: Again, being where conflicts generally are (e.g., lunch, recess, passing hall time) can help in addressing and resolving these issues before they erupt.
- Be "a fly on the wall": Many times now conflict occurs under the guise of social media or texting communication. Listening for these issues by be-

ing a "fly on the wall" can help intercept many of these Internet conflicts that are often kept on the "down low" away from parents or authority figures.

Chapter Nine

Entering the Workforce and Beyond

Growing to Adulthood

> Job training empowers people to realize their dreams and improve their lives.
> —Sylvia Mathews Burwell

CHILD PROFILE

Manny is twenty years old and is in a Structured Learning Experience (SLE) program at his public high school. He has taken a job at the local coffeehouse as a barista. While he enjoys the job, he is often late or calls out to play video games with his friends.

Manny's parents try to encourage him to go to his job, but when he does not, they often call out for him. They worry somewhat but think to themselves, "He is only twenty; he has a lifetime to work. We'll let him be a kid for now."

TAILORING THE JOB TO THE CHILD

If we want a youth to be successful in the ultimate balance of social skills and competence to adulthood, we must also provide them with jobs at which they will be relatively successful. This means finding jobs that

- they are capable of doing,
- they are able to understand,

- they are able to get to regularly, and
- if possible, demonstrate some correlation with an interest of theirs now or in the future.

TEACHING HOW TO RESPOND TO CRITICISM

It is important that a freshly minted worker begins to understand how to accept criticism. These issues are highlighted in other chapters; however, this is the ultimate test of these skills.

Can the adolescent accept criticism from supervisors or the general public? It is vital that they learn to not respond immediately and use the skills they have been taught on conflict resolution and problem solving.

SMILING AND POLITENESS CAN SURE GO A LONG WAY ...

Simply smiling and being polite and helpful are some of the easiest and most immediately applicable skills that youth can learn as they begin to work. Remembering and paralleling many of the skills that they have learned from school is crucial vocationally.

INTERNSHIPS AND VOLUNTEERING ARE KEY

Working a paid position is the ultimate test and indication of the takeoff from the landing strip of childhood toward the horizon that is adulthood. For some adolescents, the job that they take in high school may carry them to a role that will last a lifetime. Or, concurrently, it may spark an interest that allows them (with further schooling) to move toward that career path that they will follow for many years to come.

This being said, we want our children to be able to strengthen their skills at developing a work ethic. Interning or volunteering takes into account the important concepts of being dependable, punctual, and responsible in a forum that does not risk the failure of a first job. Doing so then avoids a youth's first work experience being unsuccessful and leaving a bad impression for any future opportunities ahead.

THE TECHNOLOGY OF APPLICATIONS

This is not referring to employment applications, though it is critically important for a wise adult to assist with these as well. Rather, I am referring to the host of computer programs and Internet applications that help with developing a résumé as well as securing volunteer, work, and interning opportunities.

FIRST RÉSUMÉS

Résumés have become the calling card, of sorts, for all of us to provide a summarized highlighting of our job skills. Now, most youth that are finding a first job may seem to have an anemic list of job duties. Résumés therefore, though perhaps not seeming necessary, can put a child ahead of peers because they present them as more prepared.

Volunteer, religious, and extracurricular activities that they have accomplished can serve to indicate what they have done that parallels working and the attitude and aptitude necessary. This may take some digging, which is why it is vital to do this with the youngster and be proactive in securing such experiences.

WORKING AND FRIENDSHIPS: DO THEY MIX?

For many of us, it is a fine balance between working at work and socializing at work. A person does not want to seem to be overly standoffish nor someone that is lazy and prefers to talk rather than work. This is not an easy task as it requires an ability to know the subtle overtones as to when it is okay to converse or socialize and when it is simply time to get down to work.

As our young adolescents begin to enter the workforce, there is a tendency to see this as a social outlet—which, to an extent, it is. Yet, it is vital for the success of a job that they know the balance of both.

- Be a good role model: Teach your child how, through your own example, to balance socialization and work as well as volunteering.
- Have your child volunteer: If your child volunteers, it gives them a trial attempt at what the role of work/social balance can be as well as a burgeoning understanding of work ethics.

- Use chores at home as a beginning for sharpening work ethics: Understanding that chores need to be completed before you can see friends begins a comprehension of a similar parallel when adolescents join the workforce.
- Discuss with children that socialization occurs at natural junctures: Boundaries of break times and lunch are natural junctures for which to take time off. It is important to teach youth to stick to the boundaries at these points versus socializing whenever desired.
- Teach about attendance: Teaching youth to only call out when ill and to be prompt are key commonsense traits that must be learned and respected.

THE WORLD OF DATING: THE MOST DIFFICULT CHALLENGE

What are the most awkward moments of your growing up? If you recall, it may be your first clumsy attempts at "asking someone out" or those first dates to the movies. These are the greatest tests of a child's social skills as they require them to sit with their anxiety and discomfort and still socialize. Additionally, one must understand the subtle rules and boundaries that are associated with dating, which are often not always clearly defined by adults who are equally uneasy in broaching that subject.

However, as a child becomes a teenager and then a young adult, the trajectory that you have set them on regarding this difficult subject may be vital for years to come.

Dating Should First Be Discussed to Preteens

The subject of personal space in friendships can be a natural venue into the world of dating. A youth may go from a disinterest in dating toward a greater curiosity, which should be addressed to avoid confusion. Additionally, the "birds and the bees" discussion should be started in early adolescence and continued at regular intervals.

These lessons are generally paralleled in the health classes in school in which the issue of puberty and dating becomes a part of the curriculum. That being said, this is generally only a premiere of what parents should tailor as a lesson for what they want their child(ren) to know and understand about the subject.

Group Activities

The safest way for a teen to meet others is in group activities. Many planned and group events allow for an organized function and for them to meet with others under the watchful eye of responsible adults.

As a secondary benefit, the absence of focus on the one-on-one aspect of dating takes a great deal of the anxiety off both teenagers. Rather, it allows for a more natural group dynamic of discussion and prevents lulls in conversation that are prevalent when conversational skills become lacking.

Take Time to Answer Questions

The parental role during the transition from preteen to adulthood is as significant as any other during a child's rearing. Though it is natural for them to turn away from you and seek to distance themselves through establishing friendships, a mother or father's involvement in their life is no less necessary.

When discussing these matters, take time to do so privately and seriously to get across the necessary manner of such a conversation. Be honest and answer questions concretely utilizing appropriate words and phrases. In this discussion, review boundaries of what is appropriate in dating and what is not, as well as teaching your own familial beliefs accordingly in the realm of dating.

Teach Them "No"

The conversation with younger children about "good touch" and "bad touch" should be done long before the dating conversation occurs. A good manner of doing this is to say, "No one should ever touch you anywhere that your bathing suit covers in the summer . . . nor should anyone tell you to keep a secret from your parents (except maybe a surprise party or gift)."

As an adolescent is getting into the realm of dating, this lesson needs to be reinforced by a discussion that they "own" their body and it is acceptable and prudent to say "No!" if they feel uncomfortable in any manner in regard to dating or being with another peer in that capacity. Also discuss that they have the right to keep their body private and the subsequent right to privacy.

SCHOOL APPLICATION

In many school districts, the domain of paid employment was kept separate from that of education (with the exception of some schools assisting with working papers). This is becoming less and less the case.

Now, schools recognize that those who are eighteen to twenty-one and who may have a disability must experience as seamless a transition as possible from public school to the adult world of work. Making it more complicated is that, in public school, students are "entitled" to certain services and, when they leave, they are left having to "qualify." Now schools are bridging this gap.

To help prepare students for the world of adulthood ahead some of the following interventions may be useful:

- Structured Learning Experience: These involve special education teachers whose sole job is to prepare, establish, and help students maintain employment tailored to their needs and wants. Though not every district in every state has a program similar to this, it is a critical means of assuring students don't "drop through the vocational cracks" into adulthood.
- Life skill classes: While arithmetic, reading, and history are important, some of these will have waning usage in the daily function of a child with limitations socially and/or intellectually. Therefore, programs that focus on life skills such as shopping for groceries, balancing a checkbook, developing a résumé, searching for a job, and budgeting are important to be integrated into their regular curriculum.
- Support groups: The prospective of moving on into the world and being pushed out of the warm nest of public schools can be a scary prospect for student and parent alike. Setting up support groups and/or parenting enrichment programs (either within the school or from an outside agency) can help alleviate these concerns.

Conclusion

> The most basic of all human needs is the need to understand and be understood. —Ralph Nichols

"Just wait until you get into the real world." That is an age-old mantra and warning that has been passed down from generation to generation. It is used as a warning to those who will eventually enter adulthood that the world is full of bumps, bruises, and hardships and the naïveté that is childhood does not last forever.

We try to teach our children to be ready for the world ahead by giving them every possible advantage, every tool, and every hope that they will be prepared for the environment of the future of which we will only have a glimpse, a world in which new jobs, new opportunities, and new prospects that we may not even be able to imagine will become as commonplace as smartphones or the Internet.

Sometimes, well-meaning parents try to shield their children from consequences and have them lead a comfortable life better than they had for themselves. In doing so, we must not shield them from the realities that they will experience in their lives for the consequences may be they will never develop a clear insight of how the world works. Comfort can never be prioritized over learning a life of eventual independence.

One thing that will not change is the importance of social skills and human interaction. True, it may be modified by those who choose to subvert face-to-face dialogue for that of the computer. However, ultimately, it will take conversational skills and socialization for work to be done and the soon-to-be adults to be truly fulfilled and successful.

If we are going to create a society that is the next "real world," wouldn't it be wonderful if it was one that creates successful communicators who collaborate and care about the world that they are inheriting? Would it not be great if our children looked out into a world of endless possibilities and beauty, instead of down at the glow of a smartphone like a moth fluttering around some eternal flame? A world that is better than our "real world"?

Our goal is to teach youth to have a better life than our own, a "real world" that is somehow kinder, smarter, and more inclusive of human interaction. This is the role of all of us as "life coaches" to what are ultimately all of our kids. It is the role of the teacher, the soccer coach, and, most of all, the parent.

Should you like this book, I would encourage you to read the other books I have authored by this publisher. *Parents and Teachers Working Together* details how to foster positive relationships between educators and parents. *The Likable, Effective, and Productive Educator* highlights how to attempt to juggle the many conflicting needs that educators must balance and how to not just survive but thrive as well.

Thank you for taking the time to explore with me, and I hope that this book leads you and your child/student down the long road of social skills to a place where they embrace a life that is truly fulfilling, a world, not of endless competition and comparison versus others, but one in which to be the very best me that they can be as a balanced individual.

Appendix

Essential Social Skills and Integral Components

Topic	Components
Conversational Skills	<ul><li>Learn appropriate topics to discuss.</li><li>Learn appropriate distance for conversations with respective parties.</li><li>Learn to listen and to ask open-ended questions.</li><li>Avoid talking over peers and learn taking turns.</li></ul>
Teamwork/ Cooperation	<ul><li>Work together in a practical fashion without "taking over" or not "stepping up" to do part.</li><li>Expressing emotions with no significant difficulty in controlling intense emotions for the majority of the time.</li><li>Be able to carry teamwork methods to class, recess, physical education, and lunch.</li></ul>
Ability to Utilize Additional Interpersonal Interactions	<ul><li>Be able to build acquaintance relationships to friendships.</li><li>Have knowledge of student/work boundaries in interacting correctly with others.</li><li>Be able to effectively express themselves and their needs in building friendships.</li></ul>
Self-Awareness	<ul><li>Take and accept responsibility for all facets of behaviors.</li><li>Foster, support, and use tools to maintain self-esteem.</li><li>Search for, recognize, and handle all emotional facets.</li><li>Find and use tools that can stabilize strongly negative emotions when necessary.</li></ul>

Means of Evaluating and Assessing Social-Skills Curricula

	Evaluative	Means of Assessment Formative	Summative
Why is it important to be aware of the people around you and what they are doing? Why is it vital to converse with others appropriately?	Teacher/school counselor observation	Teacher questioning, activities, and role-play	Activities, presentations, projects, role-play, and observations
When is it acceptable to ask questions? How do you express thoughts and feelings?	Teacher/school counselor observation	Teacher questioning and activities	Activities, presentations, projects, role-play, and observations
Why is it important to interact with and cooperate with other people to succeed in life? Why is it critical to demonstrate appropriate behavior when interacting with others?	Teacher/school counselor observation	Teacher questioning and activities	Activities, presentations, projects, role-play, and observations
How does a listener understand the message of others?	Teacher/school counselor observation	Teacher questioning, checklists, activities, and role-play	Activities, presentations, projects, role-play, and observations
Why is it is important to develop and maintain friendships and/or other relationships? Why is it vital to display an understanding of a person's characteristics different from your own? Why is it critical for students to learn that there can be both social and legal consequences for inappropriate behavior?	Teacher/school counselor observation	Teacher questioning, activities, and role-play	Activities, presentations, projects, role-play, and observations

	Means of Assessment		
	Evaluative	Formative	Summative
Why is it important to identify your own emotions? Why do I need to be accountable? Why is it vital to control your own impulses? Why is it crucial to be able to express anger without harming the rights of others? Why is it critical to choose an appropriate way to regulate your emotions?	Teacher/school counselor observation	Teacher questioning, checklists, activities, and role-play	Activities, presentations, projects, role-play, and observations
Why is it important to notice other people's feelings? Why is it crucial to identify basic emotions and the behaviors that accompany those emotions? How do we learn to understand and respect diversity in relationships? Why is it a priority to respond to the basic emotions of others? Why is it critical to become more understanding of the emotional needs of others?	Teacher/school counselor observation	Teacher questioning, activities, and role-play	Activities, presentations, projects, role-play, and observations
Why is it important to develop multiple social skill techniques to resolve or lessen problems? Why is it important to understand the consequences of your own actions and to accept responsibility for your own behavior? Why is it crucial to develop strategies to limit negative peer pressure? Why is it vital to resist peer pressure to perform acts that result in a reprimand? Why is it critical to accept constructive criticism?	Teacher/school counselor observation	Teacher questioning, activities, role-play, and observation	Activities, presentations, projects, role-play, and observations

Index

Anderson, Greg, 83
anger management, xii; on academic failure, 3; additional emotions blend in, 4; anxiety relationship to, 4; assertive and passive behavior in, 6, 9–10; being talked about causing, 3; child profile in, 1–2; continuum of, 7; environmental triggers of, 3; environment change for, 8; fairness understanding in, 6; humor use for, 7; hunger and tired or ill check in, 8; impulsive behaviors and, 6; interactional triggers of, 2–3; joking or sarcasm in, 2; lower threshold for, 7; music use for, 8; new places not structured causing, 3; on not being invited, 3; on overwhelming environments, 3; personal space and loudness in, 3; rudeness in, 2; rules of, 8–9; scaling of, 8; school applications in, 9–10; school discussion topics for, 10; signs and symptoms of, 5; situational triggers for, 3–4; solution searching for, 9; student handling of, 10; tunnel vision in, 5; unrecognized physical issues causing, 4; on waiting, 3; walking away from, 7

Barron, Carrie, 35
Burwell, Sylvia Mathews, 91

Carnegie Institute of Technology, 53

children: anger management profile of, 1–2; conflict resolution profile of, 83; egocentric nature of, 48; emotional aptitude of, 53; empathy profile of, 47; EQ building of, 53; extroverted characteristics of, 72–73; friendship development profile of, 71; friendship importance of, 71–72; friendship measurements of, x; hygiene awareness profile of, 65; hygiene responsibility of, 67–68; immediate feedback for, 53–54; introverted characteristics of, 72; isolated worlds of, 54; materialistic items need of, 50; "me" society of, 51; responsibility profile of, 13; responsibility role of, 28; service teaching of, 50–51; social experience involvement of, ix; social skill profile of, vii–viii, 31; social skills limited scope of, ix; tolerance profile of, 57; vocational skills profile of, 91; volunteering opportunities for, 51–52; whole village care of, ix
common interests, 37–38, 73, 80
communication, xi, xiii, 27, 36, 41, 48, 76
Concordia University, Irvine, x
conflict resolution, xii–xiii, 22–25; bystander mentality in, 88; child profile in, 83; clarifying and understanding in, 86; complaint and solution in, 85; consequences in, 88; in curriculum, 88;

deal making in, 87; educational application of, 88; emotions concerning, 86; experiencing, 84; forgiveness in, 87–88; "I" message use in, 84; issue not personality in, 87; listening and reflecting example in, 85; mood lightening in, 87; as natural life element, 83–84; role-playing for, 88
consequences, 15, 19, 69–70, 88
conversational skills, 43, 76, 77, 78, 99

dating skills, xiii; "birds and bees" discussion in, 94; group activities in, 95; parental role in, 95; personal space in, 94; privacy in, 95; rules and boundaries in, 94; saying "no" in, 95
Duke University, xi
Durlak, Joseph A., xi

educational application: for anger management, 9–10; of conflict resolution, 88; of empathy, 54–55; for friendship development, 80–81; for hygiene awareness, 70; "real" world rules for responsibility in, 21; of social skills, 44–45; for tolerance, 63; of vocational skills, 96
egocentricity, 41, 48
Elkind, David, 71
emotional intelligence (EQ or EI), 53
Emotional Intelligence (Goleman), 7, 53
empathy, xii; asking questions of others as, 54; celebrating of, 55; child profile on, 47; curricular programming for, 54–55; educational application of, 54–55; egocentricity of children regarding, 48; EQ or EI building for, 53; food pantry help fostering, 52; "giving back" importance in, 52; honesty addressing in, 47–48; immediate feedback in, 53–54; library help for, 52; modeling of, 55; notes and pictures as, 52; nursing home visit for, 52; overcoming adversity stories for, 54; philanthropic organizations involvement for, 54; religious activities for, 52; scouting opportunities for, 52; "selfie" phenomenon impacting, 49–50; service teaching for, 50–51; study percentages concerning, 49; time-tested mantra of, 47; volunteering opportunities for establishing, 51–52
EQ or EI. *See* emotional intelligence

Ford, Henry, 17
Franklin, Benjamin, ix
friendship development, x, xii; acquaintance transitioning to, 78; ask questions in, 75; childhood importance of, 71–72; child profile in, 71; common interests in, 73, 80; compliment opportunity in, 75; conversational skills for, 76, 99; conversation entering task in, 78; conversation topics for, 77; educational application for, 80–81; extracurricular school activity for, 81; extroverted characteristics in, 72–73; eye contact in, 76; good qualities for, 79–80; "I" messages in, 76; interrupting and, 76; introduction development in, 75–76; introverted characteristics in, 72; "off the table" topics in, 77–78; organized activities in, 73; parent support groups for, 73–74; play dates for, 73; positive character trait building in, 73; proper distance in, 76; "quality assess" potential relationships in, 79; reflective listening for, 76; relationship pruning in, 80; saying hello in, 75; self-defeating obstacles to, 39–41; social anxiety disorders regarding, 79; socializing reminders in, 81; "virtual friends" in, 74; "W" and "H" questions use for, 74–75; young mentor use for, 74
Frost, Robert, 1

Gandhi, Mahatma, 63
Goleman, Daniel, 7, 53

Healthline website, 9
"helicoptering" parent, 15
Holocaust Memorial Day, 61
Horan, Sean, 66
"How Technical Devices Influence Children's Brains" (Barron), 35
Huffington Post, xi, 58

hygiene awareness, xiii; assumptions about lack of, 66; child profile in, 65; concrete reminders for, 68; consistency in, 66; in curriculum, 69, 70; family affordability in, 70; first impression vital in, 66; gender-specific discussions in, 66; germ education in, 66–67; natural consequence effectiveness in, 69–70; nurse use in, 70; potential item purchase for, 69; professionals use in, 67; reasons for maintaining, 69; responsibility in, 67–68; saving face in, 68; school application of, 70; school items for, 68; skills break down in, 68; student knowledge in, 70; washing hands teaching for, 67

"I" messages, 76, 84
Internet, xiii, 58, 88, 97
introversion and extroversion, 36–37, 72–73

Jordan, Don W., xi–xii
Journal of Personality and Social Psychology Review, 49

King, Martin Luther, Jr., 63
Knox, Richard, 9
Konrath, Sara H., 49
Korda, Michael, 13

Le Metais, Joanna, xi–xii
listening, xiii, 72, 76, 85

Martin Luther King Jr. Day, 61
Mayer, John, 53
McCarthy, Kevin, 65
Mehrabian, Albert, xi
Miller, Alice, 47
Mischel, Walter, 17

New Jersey Department of Education, 59
Nichols, Ralph, 97
Nichols, Vincent, vii

parents, 15, 29, 73–74, 95
Parks, Rosa, 63
Penn State University, xi
personal space, 3, 41–42, 94

responsibility, 62; ability and competence in, 21–22; ability to assume, xiii; adult modeling of, 25; adult role in, 27–28, 28; authority figure scare results of, 18–19; capacity developing for, 25; child profile in, 13; child role in, 28; chores and tasks for, 29; classroom teaching of, 15–16; conflict resolution skill development in, 22–25; consistency and consequences in, 15, 19; developmental stages in, 22, 23; direct confrontation in, 18; educational application of "real" world rules for, 21; educational environment fostering of, 29; for emotions and actions, 26; failure and disappointment allowing in, 29; freedom and security blend in, 14; "helicoptering" parent issues in, 15; "learned helplessness" concept in, 17; marshmallow experiment for, 17; mistake belaboring in, 29; money and earning language in, 16; motivation development in, 14; for own mistakes, 29; parent involvement in, 29; physical aggression handling in, 26; positive, 29; practical application of "real" world rules for, 20; problem solving in, 26; "real" world rules for, 19; self-discipline in, 17; sincere apology learning in, 25; stating feelings in, 26
Rogers, Fred, 31

Salovey, Peter, 53
Silent Messages (Mehrabian), xi
Slate website, 58
SLE. *See* Structured Learning Experience
smartphones, x, 13, 49–50, 50, 97, 98
socialization: ability in, x; Concordia University study on, x; learning via, x–xi; work balance and, 93–94
social skills, 81; activity abandonment points in, 38–39; "adult-like", 33; all or nothing thinking in, 39; assumptions handling in, 40–41; blaming others in, 41; changing winds of, ix; child limited scope of, ix; child profile on, vii–viii, 31; classroom role models in, 44; conversation starters in, 43; curriculum development for, 45, 99–101; danger of

poor, xi; destruction of, x; educational application of, 44–45; egocentricity in, 41; foundational traits of, xii–xiii; gear shifting in, 35; as gray area, 32, 39–40; human interaction importance in, 97–98; introversion and extroversion regarding, 36–37; Jordan and Le Metais study on, xi–xii; know-it-all in, 44; Mehrabian on, xi; "on the job" training in, 34; organized activities and team building for, 44, 99; peer game interruption in, 42; peer interaction motivation in, 32–33; Penn State and Duke Universities study on, xi; persistency and giving up in, 40; personal space in, 41–42; play activity considerations in, 37; problem solving encouragement in, 45; quick redirect in, 35; raising hands as, 45; scanning environment in, 42–43; school system program considerations in, 44–45; self-defeating obstacles in, 39–41; similar interest elements in, 37–38; "simulated" practice failure of, 33; social media impacting, 35–36; student academic abilities enrichment by, xi; teaching of, 31–32; team approach in, 34–35; technology brain changes in, 35–36; unusual icebreaker use in, 43

Stewart, Rod, 6

Stöppler, Melissa Conrad, 66

Structured Learning Experience (SLE), 91, 96

"The Teen Brain: It's Just Not Grown Up Yet" (Knox), 9

tolerance, xiii; answering "why?" questions for, 62; child profile on, 57; cultural events expanding of, 59; culture sharing as, 61; educational application for, 63; encourage and share differences in, 63; foreign student mentoring in, 60; joke avoidance in, 62; as key success element, 58; learn another language as, 61; major culture religious holiday list in, 59–60; prejudice awareness in, 58–59; racial and cultural dynamics changing in, 58; self-responsibility in, 62; talk about, 61; travel as aid in, 61

vocational skills, xiii; attendance in, 94; child profile in, 91; chores as, 94; computer program use in, 93; criticism acceptance in, 92; interning or volunteering aid in, 92; job tailoring in, 91–92; life skills classes in, 96; résumés in, 93; role model in, 93; school application of, 96; SLE in, 96; smiling and politeness in, 92; socialization and work balance in, 93–94; support groups in, 96

volunteering, 51–52, 92

work ethic, 2, 16, 92, 93–94

Wright, N. T., 57

About the Author

Brett Novick holds a bachelor's degree in psychology from LaSalle University in Philadelphia and a master's degree in family therapy from Friends University in Wichita and has done postdegree work and certification in school social work at Monmouth University in New Jersey, as well as in educational leadership. Mr. Novick is licensed as a marriage and family therapist and state certified as a school social worker, supervisor, principal, and educational administrator.

He has worked as a school social worker/counselor for the past seventeen years and is an adjunct instructor at Rutgers University in New Brunswick, New Jersey. Additionally, he has been a licensed marriage and family therapist in private practice, community mental health, and substance-abuse settings over the past twenty years. He has supervised family counseling, school counseling, and centers for abused and neglected children as well as adults and children with developmental disabilities.

He has also authored nationally and internationally published articles in *American Association of Marriage and Family Therapy*, *Autism Parenting*, *National Education Digest*, *NJEA Review*, *National Association of Special Education Teachers*, *NASSP Principal Leadership*, *Better Mental Health*, and *ASCD Educational Leadership Magazine*. He has authored four additional books: *Parents and Teachers Working Together* and *The Likable, Effective, and Productive Educator*, both published by Rowman & Littlefield; *Don't Marry a Lemon*; and *Brain Bullies: Standing Up to Anxiety and Worry*.

He has been humbled by numerous awards for his work in education, inclusive education, counseling, character education, and human rights, including the NJEA Martin Luther King Jr. Human and Civil Rights Award, NJSCA Ocean County School Counselor of the Year Award, the Ocean County Mental Health Advocate Award, NJ Council on Developmental Disabilities Community Award, NJ DOE Holocaust Educator Hela Young Award, NJ DOE Inclusive Educator of the Year and Exemplary Educator Awards, NJSCA Human Rights Advocate Award, ETS/Kids Bridge Character Educator of the Year Award, and U.S. Congressional Recognition for Community Service.

www.ingramcontent.com/pod-product-compliance
Lightning Source LLC
Chambersburg PA
CBHW032029230426
43671CB00005B/250